A NEW CONSTITUTION NOW

A NEW CONSTITUTION NOW

BY

HENRY HAZLITT

New York   WHITTLESEY HOUSE   *London*
MCGRAW-HILL BOOK COMPANY, INC.

A NEW CONSTITUTION NOW

COPYRIGHT, 1942, BY THE
MCGRAW-HILL BOOK COMPANY, INC.

PRINTED IN THE UNITED STATES OF AMERICA

All rights reserved. This book, or parts thereof, may not be reproduced in any form without permission of the publishers.

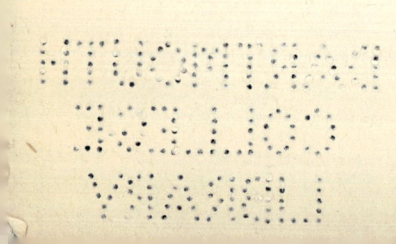

TO FRANCES

PREFACE

Since the following pages were written, an event has occurred which confirms at least one part of their thesis more sharply than any illustration cited in them. This is the President's message to Congress on Labor Day, 1942. In that document Mr. Roosevelt demanded that Congress repeal a section of the Price Control Law by Oct. 1. "In the event," he declared, "that the Congress should fail to act, and act adequately, I shall accept the responsibility, and I will act."

Now if a President can, even in the case of a single law, either successfully threaten to suspend it himself, or force Congress to repeal it because of that threat, what becomes of the powers of Congress? If a President can carry out such a threat on one occasion, on the plea of averting "a disaster which would interfere with the winning of the war," what constitutional barrier would then stand in the way of his using the same plea for whatever other power he wished to exercise, for whatever other law of Congress he wished to suspend?

The President, it will be noticed, implies that he, and not Congress, is to decide which Congressional laws "interfere with the winning of the war"; that he, and not Congress, is ultimately to decide what powers must be placed in his hands. He refuses in his Labor Day message even to indicate any definite limits to the extent of these powers. This war, he declares, "makes the use of executive power far more essential than in any previous war. . . . I cannot tell what powers may have to be exercised in order to win this war."

Now I am far from denying that in time of war the executive must be granted much wider powers than in peacetime. The executive's need for greater freedom of action in wartime is precisely one of the reasons why we need a more efficient and less rigid constitution than the one we have. The existing Constitution must be revised. But it is no less important that it be revised by constitutional means. It makes a profound difference whether the executive assumes greater powers on his own declared need for them, or whether these powers are freely granted to him by the legislative body, or directly by the people themselves. The first is the method of dictatorship; the second is the method of democracy.

Those who hold that we can simply ignore or abandon either all or part of the Constitution in time of war are confronted with the thesis of the present volume. If our existing Constitution is so inflexible and unworkable that it must be tacitly abandoned whenever the country is faced with a real crisis, of what use is it? Those who argue that, in an emergency, the constitutional balance of powers must be put aside, should candidly ask themselves whether they really believe in the Constitution as it stands.

Are they not saying in effect that it is merely a fair-weather Constitution? For what is the sense in building up "checks and balances" so elaborate and rigid that, in every crisis, we have to destroy them?

Such an arrangement is not merely pointless; it is highly dangerous. If, without revising or altering that document by the means it prescribes, we simply forget the Constitution "in order to win the war," then we are politically adrift. If we once desert, on non-constitutional grounds or by unconstitutional means, the procedures and balance of powers prescribed by the Constitution, then we not only abandon the constitutional criterion in deciding political questions; we abandon also our agreement concerning *how* those questions are to be decided and *who* is to decide them. A President may say that it is Congress's policies that "interfere with the winning of the war." But Congress may say that it is the President's policies that "interfere with the winning of the war." If he claims a super-constitutional right to set aside Congress's policies, Congress may claim a super-constitutional right to set aside his. And if such a dispute develops, who is to decide between them?

There can be only one answer: the American people. It is they who must decide. But under our Constitution, if the President and Congress disagree in a crisis, there is no way to consult the people. There is no unmistakable way to learn their verdict. Under the cabinet form of government, however, advocated in the following pages, a method for re-

PREFACE

ferring questions to the people in a crisis, if that should prove necessary, *is* provided. The people know that it is safe to grant extremely wide executive powers in wartime—provided that they, in turn, can control the executive. They need the power to change, at any time, if need be, a Congress that thwarts the executive's policies when the people approve those policies. And they need the power also to change the executive himself if he shows himself unable to carry out the national will.

In the following pages I have shown at length how and why our present constitutional system, if we adhere to it, must fail to meet an emergency. Mr. Roosevelt's Labor Day message to Congress calls attention dramatically to the opposite danger to which our present constitutional rigidity may lead— the destruction of the system itself because of sheer impatience with it, combined with a failure to provide any flexible democratic substitute.

As the history of our Latin-American neighbors must warn us, the neat balance of power contemplated by the paper theory of the presidential form of government is a state of unstable equilibrium which America has maintained up to this time almost by a miracle. The usual destiny of the presidential form of government—its tendency always in a crisis— is toward executive dictatorship. Nearly sixty years ago Woodrow Wilson saw the possibility of precisely this result.[1] And at this moment another warning,

[1] See the quotations in this book on pages 30 and 31.

PREFACE

uttered only seven years ago, seems peculiarly appropriate. It concerns the consequences of allowing

the dead hand of the past, and the difficulty of amending the Constitution, to hold us in the grip of a fatal inertia. Rome as a republic suffered from a similar rigidity in its constitutional system, a separation of powers which was ultimately resolved by civil wars and dictatorships. Always in such a crisis of constitutional development it is the stand-pat conservatives who ultimately make the destruction of the system inevitable—because they demand impossible things of antiquated machinery. It is not those who would reform but those who would ossify a constitution who bring about its destruction. They are the true begetters of fascist Caesarism.[1]

My thanks are due to Mr. Simeon Strunsky for reading proofs and for many helpful suggestions. My wife has kindly prepared the Index, and my more general debt to her help is great. I wish to express my appreciation also to the New York *Times* for allowing me to use certain material which originally appeared in its pages. I alone am responsible for the views expressed, and for whatever errors may be found.

The following publishers have generously given me their permission to quote from their books at some length: Doubleday, Doran and Company, E. P. Dutton & Co., Editorial Research Reports, Harper &

[1] W. Y. Elliott, "The Need for Constitutional Reform" (1935) pp. 207-208.

PREFACE

Brothers, Houghton Mifflin Company, The Macmillan Company, Oxford University Press, the Viking Press (B. W. Huebsch, Inc.), Whittlesey House, and the Yale University Press.

HENRY HAZLITT.

NEW YORK,
September, 1942.

CONTENTS

	PAGE
PREFACE	vii
I. OUR INFLEXIBLE CONSTITUTION	3
II. PRESIDENTIAL VS. CABINET GOVERNMENT	15
III. SOME OBJECTIONS CONSIDERED	48
IV. MORE OBJECTIONS	74
V. TOWARD THE CABINET SYSTEM	100
VI. A RESPONSIBLE GOVERNMENT IN OUTLINE: I	107
VII. A RESPONSIBLE GOVERNMENT IN OUTLINE: II	131
VIII. A RESPONSIBLE GOVERNMENT IN OUTLINE: III	165
IX. A BETTER VOTING METHOD	188
X. MINOR REFORMS	200
XI. IN THE RIGHT DIRECTION	222
XII. TO REFORM CONGRESS FROM WITHIN	241
XIII. AMENDING THE AMENDING PROCESS	251
XIV. CONCLUSION	277
INDEX	293

A NEW CONSTITUTION NOW

I

OUR INFLEXIBLE CONSTITUTION

IN JAMES BRYCE'S *American Commonwealth*, a half century ago, there appeared more than one passage that time has shown to be prophetic. After discussing some of the many grave deficiencies of our form of government, Bryce declared:

> Every European state has to fear not only the rivalry but the aggression of its neighbors. Even Britain . . . like the powers of the European Continent, must maintain her system of government in full efficiency for war as well as for peace. . . . But America lives in a world of her own. . . . Safe from attack, safe even from menace, she hears from afar the warring cries of European races and faiths. . . . Had Canada or Mexico grown to be a great power, had France not sold Louisiana, or had England, rooted on the American Continent, become a military despotism, the United States could not indulge the easy optimism which makes them tolerate the faults of their government. As it is, that which might prove to a European state a mortal disease is here nothing worse than a teasing ailment. . . . For the present, at least—it may not always be so—[America] sails upon a Summer sea.[1]

[1] Pp. 309-310.

A NEW CONSTITUTION NOW

"It may not always be so." The change that Bryce foresaw as possible has arrived. The development of the bombing plane is wiping out the security once granted by the two oceans. America finds itself in a struggle for survival against the most powerful military despotism that the world has ever known. The length and cost of this struggle—perhaps its very outcome—may depend upon whether or not we find soon enough the initiative to change our system of government to one less rigid and more responsible.

The American system of government, as compared, say, with the British, Australian or Canadian, has defects that may in ordinary times constitute merely a "teasing ailment" but could today prove a "mortal disease." We cannot make our leaders constantly accountable and responsible. We cannot force them to cooperate with each other. We cannot select or remove them at will, but only at fixed intervals.

The defects of our government have been made clear enough in the past by discerning observers like Bagehot and Bryce. The present situation only confirms their judgment. If the President and Congress disagree, there is a deadlock. Neither can appeal from the verdict of the other to that of the country. Congress cannot force the resignation of the President, as the British Parliament can that of the Prime Minister, by voting a lack of confidence. The President, on his side, cannot force Congress to adopt a policy that he considers vital by dissolving Congress and appealing from its verdict to that of the country. Congress can prevent the President from doing as he wishes but cannot make him do what it wishes. Responsibility is divided and lost even within Congress itself. The Senate can block the overwhelming will of the House, though that will may reflect an equal sentiment in the country. Worse, a single Senate committee chairman, chosen by seniority, can often block the expressed will of the House and prevent the Senate from expressing a will by his mere inaction.

The result of this system, even in quiet times, as Bryce pointed out, is that the nation does not know "how or where to fix responsibility for misfeasance or neglect," and "no one acts under the full sense of direct accountability." Under our inflexible system no issue can be taken to the country when it is urgent and uppermost. It must wait for settlement until an election date comes around two, four or six years later. Delays of that length today may prove disastrous.

Imagine what the result would be if we chose our military leaders in the field on such a principle. Suppose we elected our generals and admirals, like our Senators, for fixed periods of six years, and had no constitutional way of changing them in the meanwhile, no matter how many battles they lost or how many lives were sacrificed by their neglect or incompetence? This is no far-fetched analogy; it is very close to a statement of the actual situation. For our Commander in Chief, and the members of Congress, who together are responsible for our economic, industrial and political organization for war, and for the conduct of its grand strategy, and who choose and remove the military commanders in the field, are themselves selected for precisely such rigidly fixed periods, with no constitutional method by which the people can change them, or bring them to account, except at the end of their fixed terms.

The evils of this system are more patent today than ever before in our history. When there is a disaster like that of Pearl Harbor, almost the sole responsibility is fixed on the local commanders, who can be removed. But the responsibility of the Administration itself for appointing precisely those commanders, and for not merely tolerating but maintaining a system of divided authority between them, failed to receive the attention in the Roberts Commission report that it surely deserved.

Mr. Churchill is forced constantly to explain and defend his acts and decisions to the British people, because if at any time he fails to do this satisfactorily he can be forced to resign, as Mr. Chamberlain was forced to do before him. In this country criticism of the President is comparatively muted and indirect, chiefly for a reason that should be obvious. There is no constitutional way in which the President, if he fails to conduct the war in a manner to satisfy the country, can be forced to resign and yield to another choice.

As long as this rigid constitutional system lasts, the Presidential incumbent is our President for better or for worse until the next Presidential election day rolls around. Meanwhile, sharp criticism of the President, even if factually justified, is felt to be not merely futile but possibly dangerous, because as long as we have this constitutional rigidity there is the latent fear that such criticism may divide the country without bringing nearer the reforms that are urged.

The same sense of futility and possible danger discourages sharp criticism of Congress. When Congress takes six months to vote a disgracefully political price-control bill, there is no direct way in which the President can bring it to account, and no immediate way in which the people can bring it to account. The President cannot threaten to dissolve a recalcitrant Congress that refuses to take vitally necessary measures in time. The people cannot recall its members. It will be four years, indeed, before some of them can be held accountable.

Our analogy of irremovable generals in the field could be extended. Suppose that our troops were led by three different generals, any one of whom could countermand the orders of the other, but no one of whom could bring about the removal of the other, and no one of whom had final authority or could make the final decision on strategy? In America and England there has lately been a great deal of justified insistence on a unified command in the military sphere. It is even more important that there should be a "unified command," a unified leadership, in the governmental organization that is superior to and responsible for the military. In each case the lack of such unified leadership must lead to confusion of policy and paralysis of action. In each case the lack of unified leadership must make it impossible to know where to fix responsibility for what is done badly or what is not done at all.

Our Constitution, at the time it was adopted, was a document far in advance of its age. Even today there could be no nobler statement of part of our war aims than one particular part of that Constitution, the Bill of Rights. But that part of our Constitution which deals with the mere *machinery* of government must now be candidly reexamined in the light of the present crisis.

2

The Constitution exists for the country, not the country for the Constitution. We must not make a fetish of a rigid legal document. We cannot permit ourselves to lose this war, or even to prolong this war, merely because we have become too hidebound to reexamine and to change that document. We must be at least as ready to make progressive changes in government as our forefathers were when they framed our basic law. No one today thinks that the proper way to show our admiration for the Wright brothers' original biplane would have been never to design anything better. Nor is this the way to show our admiration for the enterprise of the men who framed the Constitution. One of them, James Madison, remarked in *The Federalist* (No. 43): "That useful alterations will be suggested by experience could not but be foreseen." Although he wished to guard against "that extreme facility which would render the Constitution too mutable," he thought it well to guard also against "that extreme difficulty which might perpetuate its discovered faults."

What are the alterations in our Constitution that experience has suggested—that experience has shown, indeed, now to be imperative? It is not difficult to draw their main outlines. The government must be responsible and accountable at all times to the people. This means that the people must have potential control of their government at all times, and not simply at rigid election dates two or four years apart. The people must have the power, in short, to change their government at any time and, if necessary, to change it completely.

To make this practically possible, Congress should have power at any time to vote a lack of confidence in the Executive, who would then have the choice of resigning or of dissolving Congress. In the latter case, he would force every member of Congress to go to the country for reelection, and himself go for such reelection. If the Executive won the country's verdict, he would get a Congress pledged to support him; if he lost it, the new Congress could itself choose a new leader.

There is no use trying to disguise the fact that a complete reform of this sort would involve a very extensive change in our whole method of government. The present method of choosing our real Chief Executive would change; it would be like that of choosing a prime minister. And the present method of electing Congress would change. Either Senators would have to be made subject to election at any time, like a reformed House, with their present system of six-year overlapping terms discontinued, or, preferably, the powers of the Senate would have to be curbed so that it could not thwart the will of the House on major issues. To ensure the proper quality of Representatives and Senators, the present rigid requirement that each must be a resident of the State from which he is elected should be abolished. Other changes of a less radical nature would be needed. One important change, a corollary of popular control, would be to permit at least a limited form of recall by the voters of his district or State of any particular Representative or Senator.

The merit of a constitutional system of this sort is not merely that it would empower the people to remove its leaders at any time that these proved unable to carry out the national will. The mere existence of such a power on the part of the people would also have a salutary effect on the responsiveness to the national will of those leaders already in office. It would tend equally to make the existing opposition party in Congress more responsible in its opposition, and force it to become positive rather than merely obstructive in its program. For the effectiveness of this opposition would depend upon its ability to convince the country that it was a conceivable alternative to the existing administration and that it was fit to govern.

3

Such a thoroughgoing revision of our Constitution has now become imperative if we are to meet today's terribly urgent problems. But the present writer recognizes equally the cold fact that there is little opinion in this country at the present time to support what will seem to many so radical a change. Even if there were already a widespread sentiment for it, there would still probably be the widest differences of opinion regarding the details of such a change. A situation could conceivably arise, however, in which the position of the country suddenly became so perilous that public opinion, in order to surmount it, would either ignore the Constitution or demand in a single hasty step a radical revision that had received little study. If we act soon enough, we can avoid either the need or the excuse for such precipitate action. It is far more desirable, if time permits, to achieve our goal by at least two separate steps. Fortunately, the first of these is a change that we can feel confident the American people would support immediately if it were presented to them. This is a change in the method of amending the Constitution as now provided in Article V.

What we must do is to remove the present ambiguities, inordinate difficulties and prohibitive delays and permit a method of amendment that could be used in a crisis. The best method that suggests itself is the one already in use in the Commonwealth of Australia. Amendments to the Constitution of that country may be proposed by a vote of an absolute majority of both houses.[1] The proposed amendments

[1] Australia has a Senate and a House of Representatives after our own model.

are then submitted to a direct vote of the people, and adopted if they are approved by a majority of the voters in a majority of the States. It is obvious that, if this method of amendment were once established, it would be possible to amend our own Constitution, if necessary, in a few months at most.

Australian experience has not shown that such a simplification of the amending process would lead to constitutional change with undue haste or for frivolous reasons. Since the adoption of the Australian Constitution, though the Australian Parliament has proposed some eighteen amendments, only three have been accepted by the people.

Because Congress could not be depended upon to propose any amendment that would have the effect of reducing any of its own powers or prerogatives, it would probably be desirable to supplement this method by allowing state legislatures also to propose amendments, as, indeed, Article V already ostensibly does. But instead of leaving this, as now, a dead letter by its vagueness and sheer clumsiness, we might compel Congress to submit a proposed amendment to the people if, say, one-fourth of the state legislatures propose such an amendment within any period of three years.

If the amendatory clause of the Constitution were amended in this way, the change would instantly improve the health and flexibility of our democracy. The people would feel that their government was much more nearly in their control, or at least that they could bring it within control without excessive difficulty. We should be free to consider seriously amendments to the Constitution that are not now considered, not because they lack merit but solely because the institutional barriers to amendments are so great.

Not the least important reason for making it simpler to amend our Constitution is that the excessive difficulties now in the way give some of our leaders an excuse for urging that, instead of submitting honest amendments upon which the people may then have an opportunity to express themselves directly, we should "interpret" the existing Constitution to mean that these officials already have the new powers they are looking for. When our constitutional inflexibility becomes an excuse for usurpation of powers not clearly granted, then it has lost its purpose, even from the most conservative point of view.

To make our Constitution flexible is as important to winning the war as price controls, priorities, taxes and many other essential measures. We have now learned from the report of the Roberts Commission on the disaster at Pearl Harbor, how bad military organization, such as a divided authority between Army and Navy, can lose a battle and almost lose a war. How much more important, then, to success in war is the organization at the top—the organization above that of the Army and Navy and Air Force on the actual battle fronts. If that organization is itself plagued by divided authority, if we do not know where to place responsibility for failure to take proper action in time, because the Senate and House and President are all able to nullify each other's will, we can lose the war, or we can lose at best precious time and treasure, and sacrifice needlessly thousands of American lives, simply because someone who cannot be held to instant account fails to do something somewhere along the line of the complicated constitutional process.

Our present system of government, in sum, is anachronistic, inflexible, and irresponsible. It is dangerously inefficient even in time of peace and fatally inadequate for total war.

It is sometimes said, perhaps too facilely, that the cure for the evils of democracy is more democracy. Here is at least one case where that aphorism clearly applies. The only true democracy is one that allows the people to change their governmental leaders the moment they find it necessary to do so—and above all to change them in a crisis. To simplify and improve the amending process to the Constitution is both desirable in itself and a necessary first step in this direction. It is a step that should be taken without delay.

II

PRESIDENTIAL vs. CABINET GOVERNMENT

THE grave defects in our Constitution, as I have just endeavored to show, are in large part responsible for our failure to organize efficiently for the conduct of the war. It may be thought that under the stress of the present crisis I have exaggerated those defects. On the contrary, the peculiar need for temperate internal discussion while a total war is in progress has led me to state the existing defects of our Constitution with restraint. For the particular criticisms that I have made, in fact, I cannot even claim originality. They are criticisms offered more than three-quarters of a century ago by John Stuart Mill and by the most penetrating analyst of political constitutions in modern times, Walter Bagehot. And they have been repeated and confirmed since their day, in times of quiet as well as times of crisis, by Woodrow Wilson, by Viscount Bryce, and by a series of coolheaded students of our institutions, both foreign and American.

I should like to call attention to some of these criticisms here. If the present chapter seems more like an anthology than an original composition, I am sure most readers will not object. The superior merits of the British cabinet over the American presidential system have been argued by men with better opportunities for close observation than I and with far more persuasive pens than mine. I see no reason why I should not take full advantage of that fact.

I begin with a quotation from John Stuart Mill's *Representative Government*, published in 1861:

> There ought not to be any possibility of that deadlock in politics which would ensue on a quarrel breaking out between a President and an Assembly, neither of whom, during an interval which might amount to years, would have any legal means of ridding itself of the other. To get through such a period without a *coup d'état* being attempted, on either side or on both, requires such a combination of the love of liberty and the habit of self-restraint as very few nations have yet shown themselves capable of: and though this extremity were avoided, to expect that the two authorities would not paralyze each other's operations is to suppose that the political life of the country will always be pervaded by a spirit of mutual forbearance and compromise, imperturbable by the passions and excitements of the keenest party struggles. Such a spirit may exist, but even where it does there is imprudence in trying it too far.[1]

The United States (unless we set down the Civil War as a frightful exception) has until now shown that rare "combination of the love of liberty and the habit of self-restraint" which Mill found essential for peaceful presidential government. But it is virtually the only country that has done so. Nearly all our

[1] Everyman ed., p. 338.

Latin-American neighbors who have done us the honor of imitating our form of government have suffered from a seemingly endless cycle of dictatorship and revolution. Some British writers on South America maintain that this dictatorship-revolution cycle has been the direct result of the presidential system.[1] No doubt this overstates the case. Reading the chapters Inevitable Dictators and The Outlook for Democracy in Duncan Aikman's *The All-American Front*, for example, leads one to wonder how *any* form of democratic government can hope to be successful under the conditions that prevail in most Latin-American countries. But one conclusion does emerge clearly: that generations of the presidential form of government have done almost nothing to cure these conditions or to educate the South American countries politically. There is every reason to suppose that cabinet government would have proved incomparably superior in this respect. Certainly it could not have shown a more complete record of failure.

Walter Bagehot's great book *The English Constitution* was published in 1867. It was the first volume to recognize and make clear the real nature of that constitution in its modern development. Bagehot, as Lord Balfour has remarked, looked at contemporary political institutions closely and for himself.

The efficient secret of the English Constitution,

[1] See, for example, ERNEST HAMBLOCH, *His Majesty the President of Brazil* (1936): "There is one feature common to the constitutional law of republics in the continent of America, *viz.* the autocracy of the Head of the State. Indeed, the essential characteristic of those republican charters of liberty is that they grant letters of marque to the president of the republic."—From the Preface.

Bagehot saw, was "the close union, the nearly complete fusion, of the executive and legislative powers." Before he wrote, the traditional theory was that the goodness of the British Constitution consisted in the entire separation of the legislative and executive authorities; but in truth, as he saw, its merit consisted in their singular approximation. The connecting link, he found, was the *Cabinet*, which he seems to have been the first to describe clearly as "a committee of the legislative body selected to be the executive body." The Prime Minister, the real head of the nation, though not elected as such directly by the people, was elected by the representatives of the people. He was an example of "double election" (as our own President still is in theory, though never in practice). Bagehot also pointed out that the "legislature chosen, in name, to make laws, in fact finds its principal business in making and in keeping an executive." The essential characteristic of the Cabinet is that it should be chosen by the legislature out of persons agreeable to and trusted by the legislature. "Naturally these are principally its own members—but they need not be exclusively so."

Now this committee of the legislature has one extraordinary power that is the principal secret of its effectiveness. "It is a committee which can dissolve the assembly which appointed it." It can appeal from the judgment of the parliament to the verdict of the people. It can ask the voters *at any time* to decide through new elections whether on a particular major issue the majority in the existing parliament, or the cabinet, has its approval. "The English system, therefore, is not an absorption of the executive power by the legislative power; it is a fusion of the two. Either the cabinet legislates and acts, or else it can dissolve. It is a creature, but it has the power of destroying its creators. It is an executive which can annihilate the legislature, as well as an executive which is the nominee of the legislature."

The democratic competitor of this system is the presidential system, the characteristic of which is that "the President is elected from the people by one process, and the House of Representatives by another. The independence of the legislative and executive powers is the specific quality of the presidential government, just as their fusion and combination is the precise principle of Cabinet government."

The separation of the legislative and executive (and judicial) arms of the American Government, I may add at this point, was not accidental but designed. It was based on a misunderstanding by the Founding Fathers of the real nature of the British Constitution—a misunderstanding not difficult to account for, because the modern British Constitution had not yet evolved. The real British executive at the time that our own Constitution was framed was not a prime minister chosen by the representatives of the people; he was still an hereditary monarch. George III chose and dismissed his own ministers. It was natural that our forefathers, when they came to frame our Constitution, should unconsciously regard the executive as an alien and outside force, and should come to think that liberty rested on the complete independence of the legislature from the executive. This natural inclination was strengthened by the influence of the theories of the French political philosopher Montesquieu, in his *Esprit de Lois* (1748), in which he originated the venerable principle of "the separation of powers," declaring: "There can be no liberty where the legislative and executive powers are united in the same person, or body of magistrates." [1]

Bagehot was the first to make clear the impracticability of the doctrine of separation of powers. (Madison and other members of the American Constitutional Convention, it is true, sensed that impracticability, though only when the doctrine was carried to a more extreme form than in the Constitution they helped to frame.) "If the persons who have to do the work," Bagehot pointed out, "are not the same as those who have to make the laws, there will be a controversy between the two sets of persons. . . . The executive becomes unfit for its name since it cannot execute what it decides on; the legislature is demoralized by liberty, by taking decisions of which others (and not itself) will suffer the effects." The great defect of the American system is not merely that it can bring deadlock between Congress and the President (not to speak of deadlock between the two houses of Congress) but that it usually becomes impossible to fix the precise responsibility for that deadlock or to do anything about resolving it. "When a

[1] See the discussion of Montesquieu and the doctrine of separation of powers by JAMES MADISON, *The Federalist*, No. 47 (1788).

difference of opinion arises, the legislature is forced to fight the executive, and the executive is forced to fight the legislature; and so very likely they contend to the conclusion of their respective terms."

"Cabinet government," Bagehot went on to point out, "educates the nation; the presidential does not educate it, and may corrupt it."[1] "It has been said that England invented the phrase, 'Her Majesty's Opposition'; that it was the first government which made a criticism of administration as much a part of the polity as administration itself." A debate in Parliament may immediately determine the decision on a great issue, and consequently everyone who participates in it, because his own political future may also be then and there involved, uses every faculty to present his case with as great effect as possible. There is

[1] For convenience, I have adopted throughout the present volume the designations of the two types of government traditional since Bagehot's day, referring to the American system nearly always as the "presidential" and to the English sometimes as the "parliamentary" and sometimes as the "cabinet" system. There is some danger in the use of these designations, however, unless the reader recognizes from the beginning that they are arbitrary labels and are not to be taken too seriously as descriptions. The "presidential" system could just as well be—and sometimes is—called the "congressional," thus emphasizing its legislative rather than its executive side. The most accurate designation would doubtless be the "presidential-congressional" system, for this would include both aspects and also emphasize the division between them. But this label would be far too clumsy and annoying to carry through a whole book. The traditional terminology tends, if anything, to create a bias in favor of the "presidential" over the "parliamentary" system for the same reason that a single executive can always arouse more popular enthusiasm than a many-headed legislature. The reader should always bear in mind, therefore, that we are by no means contrasting "executive" with "legislative" government. Just as the "presidential" system could with equal propriety be called the "congressional," so the "parliamentary" system could with equal justice be named the "premier" system.

no equal incentive behind the debates in Congress, and no equal incentive for public interest in them. Bagehot's discussion of this point is so interesting, and though written in 1867 so much of it is still applicable, that it bears quotation at length:

Human nature despises long arguments which come to nothing—heavy speeches which precede no motion—abstract disquisitions which leave visible things where they were. But all men heed great results, and a change of government is a great result. It has a hundred ramifications; it runs through society; it gives hope to many, and it takes away hope from many. It is one of those marked events which, by its magnitude and its melodrama, impress men even too much. And debates which have this catastrophe at the end of them—or may so have it—are sure to be listened to, and sure to sink deep into the national mind.

Travelers even in the Northern States of America, the greatest and best of presidential countries, have noticed that the nation was "not specially addicted to politics"; that they have not a public opinion finished and chastened as that of the English has been finished and chastened. A great many hasty writers have charged this defect on the "Yankee race," on the Anglo-American character; but English people, if they had no motive to attend to politics, certainly would not attend to politics. At present there is *business* in their attention. They assist at the determining crisis; they assist or help it. Whether the government will go out or remain is determined by the debate, and by the division in parliament. And the opinion out of doors, the secret pervading disposition of society, has a great influence on that division.

PRESIDENTIAL VS. CABINET GOVERNMENT

The nation feels that its judgment is important, and it strives to judge. It succeeds in deciding because the debates and the discussions give it the facts and the arguments. But under a presidential government a nation has, except at the electing moment, no influence; it has not the ballot-box before it; its virtue is gone, and it must wait till its instant of despotism again returns. It is not incited to form an opinion like a nation under a cabinet government; nor is it instructed like such a nation. There are doubtless debates in the legislature, but they are prologues without a play. There is nothing of a catastrophe about them; you cannot turn out the government. The prize of power is not in the gift of the legislature, and no one cares for the legislature. The executive, the great center of power and place, sticks irremovable; you cannot change it in any event. The teaching apparatus which has educated our public mind, which prepares our resolutions, which shapes our opinions, does not exist. No presidential country needs to form daily, delicate opinions, or is helped in forming them.

It might be thought that the discussions in the press would supply the deficiencies in the constitution; that by a reading people especially, the conduct of their government would be as carefully watched, that their opinions about it would be as consistent, as accurate, as well considered, under a presidential as under a cabinet polity. But the same difficulty oppresses the press which oppresses the legislature. It can *do nothing*. It cannot change the administration; the executive was elected for such and such years, and for such and such years it must last. People wonder that so literary a people as the Americans—a people who read more than any people who ever lived, who read so many newspapers—should

A NEW CONSTITUTION NOW

have such bad newspapers. The papers are not so good as the English, because they have not the same motive to be good as the English papers. At a political "crisis," as we say—that is, when the fate of an administration is unfixed, when it depends on a few votes, yet unsettled, upon a wavering and veering opinion—effective articles in great journals become of essential moment. *The Times* has made many ministries. When, as of late, there has been a long continuance of divided parliaments, of governments which were without "brute voting power," and which depended on intellectual strength, the support of the most influential organ of English opinion has been of critical moment. If a Washington newspaper could have turned out Mr. Lincoln, there would have been good writing and fine argument in the Washington newspapers. But the Washington newspapers can no more remove a president during his term of place than *The Times* can remove a lord mayor during his term of office. Nobody cares for a debate in Congress which "comes to nothing," and no one reads long articles which have no influence on events. The Americans glance at the heads of news, and through the paper. They do not enter upon a discussion. They do not *think* of entering upon a discussion which would be useless.[1]

It may be urged that intelligent American interest in politics, the quality of the American press, and the quality of American public opinion have all improved greatly since these words were written seventy-five years ago. This is true; but the improvement in some directions has been more seeming than real. In a total war like the present, when every decision of the gov-

[1] WALTER BAGEHOT, *The English Constitution* (1867), World's Classic's ed., pp. 18-20.

ernment may have a profound and immediate effect upon our daily lives, it is hardly conceivable that there should not be intense interest in governmental decisions. Nevertheless, the constitutional restrictions on what the American people are able to *do*, affect what it is prudent for them to *say*, and this in turn unconsciously affects even what they dare to *think*. If the President turns out not to be the man best fitted to lead the country in a successful prosecution of a war, if he bungles critical decisions badly and to the national cost, men fear to say so plainly. There is no immediate constitutional method of changing the executive, as there is in England. Therefore patriotic men fear that criticism which brings responsibility home too closely to the President can only divide the country without affecting the change necessary. But this fear, only partly conscious, has a further effect: it leads men to wishful thinking; it leads them to tell themselves that the situation cannot be as bad as all that, and that the necessary changes can be effected by moderate arguments which do not urge a change in government but merely in the policies adopted by the existing government. Such a belief will continue to be held even though experience shows that the existing government will not modify its major policies, and may not even, however willing, know how to adopt and carry out the proper policies. The limitations imposed by a rigid constitution, in short, may pervert a nation's very thinking, leading it to a sort of national neurosis in which it refuses to face the truth about the situation that confronts it.

Continuing to press his criticism, Bagehot argued not only that the American system encourages deadlocks between the executive and the legislature, and fails properly to educate public opinion, but that it tends, as compared with the cabinet system, to elect inferior men to office. One reason why Congressmen tend to be inferior to members of Parliament is that election to Congress offers far less chance of later promotion for an able man than does election to Parliament. A member of Parliament may nourish the hope, even during his first term, of being chosen for the Cabinet; such a prize seems always possible. No similar prize attaches to election to Congress.

"Unless a member of the legislature," wrote Bagehot, "be sure of something more than speech, unless he is incited by the hope of action, and chastened by the chance of responsibility, a first-rate man will not care to take the place, and will not do much if he does take it." Another kind of difficulty, he thought, affected our method of choosing presidents. The method of nomination by political conventions tended in most cases to become nomination by political wire pullers. The English Prime Minister is chosen by his colleagues in Parliament, who know his qualities intimately; usually he has spent some years as the leader of his party in Parliament when it was in the minority, or as a member of the Cabinet when his party was previously in power. His colleagues know what he will do, because they know what he has done. He is in nearly all cases, for the same reasons, a man whose record is known to the country.

PRESIDENTIAL VS. CABINET GOVERNMENT

But presidential conventions often nominate "dark horses"—the selection of what Bagehot called "an unknown quantity." Even if the Americans scored an occasional success in such a lottery, he insisted, this was no argument for lotteries. Moreover, he pointed out, the very gifts that a particular statesman may have to rule in one set of circumstances may unfit him for rule in other circumstances. "By the structure of the world we often want, at the sudden occurrence of a grave tempest, to change the helmsman— to replace the pilot of the calm by the pilot of the storm." Summing up his indictment of the American system, Bagehot declared:

> The American government calls itself a government of the supreme people; but at a quick crisis, the time when a sovereign power is most needed, you cannot *find* the supreme people. You have got a Congress elected for one fixed period, going out perhaps by fixed installments, which cannot be accelerated or retarded—you have a President chosen for a fixed period, and immovable during that period: all the arrangements are for *stated* times. There is no *elastic* element, everything is rigid, specified, dated. Come what may, you can quicken nothing and can retard nothing. You have bespoken your government in advance, and whether it suits you or not, whether it works well or works ill, whether it is what you want or not, by law you must keep it.[1]

2

Eighteen years after the appearance of Bagehot's unsparing analysis of the defects of our own Consti-

[1] *Ibid.*, pp. 26-27.

tution as compared with the English, there appeared in America a small volume by a young author of twenty-eight. It was entitled *Congressional Government*, and it had been written as a doctorate thesis. The author's name was Woodrow Wilson.

The volume was that of a young man who had been clearly influenced by Bagehot's analysis. But it was also the book of a man who had looked at our institutions at first hand and for himself. Woodrow Wilson's volume did not directly advocate constitutional revision. He insisted that he was merely "pointing out facts—diagnosing, not prescribing remedies." But on every page he makes clear his preference for the English cabinet system over the American congressional system. The most insistent criticism that he made of the workings of our system, which concerns the internal organization of Congress itself, can best be considered at a later point. What it is important to notice here is the author's attack on the "undiscriminating and almost blind worship" of the Constitution. He saw, however, or thought he saw, that the people of his own generation were "the first Americans to hear our own countrymen ask whether the Constitution is still adapted to serve the purposes for which it was intended." And he ended by declaring: "The Constitution is not honored by blind worship. . . . The first step towards emancipation from the timidity and false pride which have led us to seek to thrive despite the defects of our national system rather than seem to deny its perfection is a fearless criticism of that system."

Woodrow Wilon reserved his own most vigorous criticism of our constitutional system for his chapter The Executive. Our President, he declared, was, in effect, "elected" by the convention of the dominant party, for the choice of that convention was "practically equivalent to election, and might as well be called election by any one who is writing of broad facts, and not of fine distinctions." This meant, however, an absurd situation under which the President is elected by a representative body "which has nothing to do with him after his election." Wilson quoted with approval the proposal of Roger Sherman at the Constitutional Convention of 1787, who held that as the executive is "nothing more than an institution for carrying the will of the legislature into effect," he "ought to be appointed by, and accountable to, the legislature only."

Wilson ridiculed, also, the President's rigidly fixed term of office:

Nothing short of a well-nigh impossible impeachment can unmake a President, except four successions of the seasons. . . . A Prime Minister must keep himself in favor with the majority, a President need only keep alive. . . .

Great crimes such as might speed even impeachment are not ordinary things in the loosest public service. . . . That which usually and every day clogs and hampers good government is folly or incapacity on the part of the ministers of state. Even more necessary, therefore, than a power clothed with authority to accuse, try, and punish for public crime is some ultimate authority, whose privilege it shall be to dismiss for inefficiency. Impeachment is aimed altogether above the head of business management. A merchant would not think it fair, even if it were lawful, to shoot a clerk who could not learn the business. Dismissal is quite as effective for his purposes, and more merciful to the clerk. The crying inconvenience of our system is, therefore, that the constitutional authority whose prerogative it is to direct policy and oversee administration has fewer facilities for getting its work well done than has the humblest citizen for obtaining satisfactory aid in his own undertakings.

The investigatory powers of Congress, Wilson continued, were usually ineffective. Suppose that a congressional committee unearths a scandal involving a member of the Cabinet?

After all is over and the murder out, probably nothing is done. The offenders, if any one has offended, often remain in office, shamed before the world, and ruined in the estimation of all honest people, but still drawing their salaries and comfortably waiting for the short memory of the public mind to forget them. Why unearth the carcass if you cannot remove it?

Finally, summing up the major defects of our Constitution, Wilson declared:

It is impossible to deny that this division of authority and concealment of responsibility are calculated to subject the government to a very distressing paralysis in moments of emergency. . . . Congress must act through the President and his Cabinet; the President and his Cabinet must wait upon the will of Congress. There is no one supreme, ultimate head—whether magistrate or representative body—which can decide at once and with conclusive authority what shall be done at those times when some decision there must be, and that immediately. Of course this lack is of a sort to be felt at all times, in seasons of tranquil rounds of business as well as moments of sharp crisis; but in times of sudden exigency it might prove fatal—fatal either in breaking down the system or in failing to meet the emergency.

The first of these two possible consequences, Wilson added in a footnote, was precisely what did happen in the Civil War: "The Constitution had then to stand aside that President Lincoln might be as prompt as the seeming necessities of the time."
While it is "manifestly a radical defect in our federal system that it parcels out power and confuses responsibility as it does," Woodrow Wilson feared that "the main purpose of the Convention of 1787 seems to have been to accomplish this grievous mistake." The "literary theory" of checks and balances, he thought, is simply a consistent account of what our constitution makers tried to do: those checks and balances have proved mischievous just to the extent to which they have succeeded in establishing themselves as realities. But Wilson thought it "quite safe to say that were it possible to call together again the members of that wonderful Convention to view the work of their hands in the light of the century that has tested it, they would be the first to admit that the only fruit of dividing power had been to make it irresponsible."

The cure that the future President recommended was implicit in his criticism:

> If there be one principle clearer than another, it is this: that in any business, whether of government or of mere merchandizing, *somebody must be trusted*, in order that when things go wrong it may be quite plain who should be punished. . . . *Power and strict accountability for its use* are the essential constituents of good government. . . . The best rulers are always those to whom great power is intrusted in such a manner as to make them feel that they will surely be abundantly honored and recompensed for a just and patriotic use of it, and to make them know that nothing can shield them from full retribution for every abuse of it.[1]

3

In 1888, three years after the publication of *Congressional Government*, there appeared the first edition of a volume that was to receive far more fame, by an author who was to receive somewhat less. It was *The American Commonwealth*, by James Bryce. The book was the product of many years of research and firsthand study. Bryce was a Scotsman of brilliant literary and political gifts. He made the first of his series of visits to America in 1870. He began to work on *The American Commonwealth* in 1883. He was not named British Ambassador here until 1907, but by that time he had already paid seven visits to this country; and he utilized his increasing experience

[1] Most of these quotations are from the chapter The Executive in *Congressional Government* (1885).

and knowledge, as well as the later unrivaled opportunities of his six years as Ambassador, in the successive editions of the volumes that were published during a quarter of a century. For his volume was not only the first important all-round study of our political institutions—with the exception of Alexis de Tocqueville's—but because of its penetration, thoroughness and balance remains a classic in its field to this day.

It is remarkable how closely the criticism of the American Constitution by Bryce, after years of first-hand study, parallels that made more than two decades previously by Bagehot. The Fathers of the Constitution, he points out, though admiring British institutions—with the exception of the hereditary principle—as providing the foundations for freedom, failed to adopt the English cabinet system "because they did not know of its existence. They did not know of it because it was still immature, because Englishmen themselves had not understood it, because the recognized authorities did not mention it." Following Locke, Blackstone and Montesquieu, they thought that the secret of the British Constitution rested on the separation of the executive, legislative and judicial powers:

> They divided the legislature from the executive so completely as to make each not only independent, but weak even in its own proper sphere. The President was debarred from carrying Congress along with him, as a popular prime minister may carry Parliament, to effect some sweeping change. . . . He is forbidden to appeal at a crisis from Congress to the country. . . . Congress

on the other hand was weakened, as compared with the British Parliament in which one House has become dominant, by its division into two co-equal houses, whose disagreement paralyzes legislative action. . . . The nation does not always know how or where to fix responsibility for misfeasance or neglect. The persons and bodies concerned in making and executing the laws are so related to one another that each can generally shift the burden of blame on some one else, and no one acts under the full sense of direct accountability. . . . [Congress], in ordinary times, lacks great leaders, and the most obvious cause why it lacks them, is its disconnection from the executive. . . . Congress cannot guide or stimulate the President, nor replace him by a man fitter for the emergency.

It may be replied by persons whose memories are short, or who have not troubled to study closely the effect of our political organization upon our political decisions, that all these defects, however much of an inconvenience or a nuisance they may be, have at least done no great harm—have so far, at least, led to no great disaster. But this is certainly a conclusion open to serious doubt. The American rejection of membership in the League of Nations and in the World Court, and our failure to participate in any effort toward the postwar stabilization and pacification of Europe, were obviously connected with the requirement of a two-thirds vote in the Senate for ratification of treaties, as well as with that separation of powers which made it impossible for President Wilson to speak with authority regarding the policy of his Government, however much Europe may have thought that he was doing so. European statesmen could not understand the action of "America" in rejecting the very League of Nations and some of the very peace terms that they had been forced to accept by "America." They accused us of a flagrant breach of faith. They forgot that the President did not have the power to speak for Congress as a British prime minister has the power to speak for Parliament. If Wilson could have dissolved Congress and appealed to the country by an immediate election on the specific issue of the League of Nations, I believe he would have won.[1] But no clear-cut election on that issue ever took place, and the question of what the actual verdict would have been must remain forever unanswered. If America *had* participated in the postwar settlement, however, the whole disaster of Hitlerism and the present war could have been averted. Apparently small causes—"a mere change in governmental machinery"—may sometimes have enormous effects.

It is the opinion of Bryce, to cite another example, that the defects of the American Government may even have been responsible for our Civil War:

> Inevitable the struggle may have been; and in its later stages passion had grown so hot, and the claims of the slaveholders so extravagant, that possibly under no scheme of government—so some high American authorities hold—could a peaceful solution have been looked

[1] *Cf.* CLARENCE A. BERDAHL, "Myths about the Peace Treaties of 1919-20," *The American Scholar* (Summer, 1942), pp. 261-274.

for. Yet it must be remembered that the carefully devised machinery of the Constitution did little to solve that problem or avert that struggle, while the system of divided and balanced and limited powers, giving every advantage to those who stood by the existing law, and placing the rights of the States behind the bulwarks of an almost unalterable instrument, may have tended to aggravate the spirit of uncompromising resistance. The nation asserted itself at last, but not till the resources which the Constitution provided for the attainment of a peaceful solution had irretrievably failed.[1]

Surely it is time now to revise our constitutional arrangements before they involve us in new and greater disasters.

4

The arguments of Bagehot, Wilson and Bryce, powerful as they were, had amazingly little effect on American thought, so complacent did we remain regarding the virtues of our Constitution. But a few Americans, at least, have spoken out boldly, and with somewhat less politeness than our ablest foreign critics have thought necessary. In 1921, for example, there was published a volume by William MacDonald, *A New Constitution for a New America*. With the exception of South America, MacDonald declared, where the various republics have so freely copied from our own practices, "no constitutional arrangement so lacking in flexibility" as that of the United States "is now to be found anywhere in the world":

[1] All the quotations of Bryce in this section are from Chaps. XXV and XXVI of *The American Commonwealth*.

PRESIDENTIAL VS. CABINET GOVERNMENT

The United States has possessed from the beginning a national government two of whose three departments are cast in rigid chronological molds, with the result that they are beyond the reach even of organized public opinion, save at stated intervals at which elections are required to take place. While on the one hand the people are powerless to change the personnel of their national government whenever, unhappily, it may have ceased to represent them properly, they are on the other hand compelled to vote at stated periods on the question of change whether or not at the moment a change is desired.[1]

This statement of twenty years ago directs attention to the dilemma that American voters face in November, 1942, a dilemma caused solely by the inflexible nature of our Constitution and its arbitrary division of the executive from the legislative branch. After November we cannot hold another Congressional election for two years, no matter what crisis develops in the meanwhile. But we must hold a Congressional election in November *whether the country wants to hold such an election or not.*

Consider the dilemma that may be faced by the majority of the voters. If they approve the Administration's domestic policy and its conduct of the war, they need merely reelect Democratic majorities. In such a case no harm will be done, but neither will any particular good result: the election will simply have been unnecessary. Suppose, however, that the majority of voters should strongly disapprove the

[1] WILLIAM MACDONALD, *A New Constitution for a New America* (1921), p. 17.

Administration's economic policy or its conduct of the war. What are they to do then? They cannot change the Administration itself. They cannot change the President and his Cabinet. They cannot even change more than a third of the Senate. They can only change the House of Representatives.

The Democrats will doubtless argue in the campaign that, if the people elect a Republican Congress, Congress will not follow the President's leadership but only produce a deadlock. The Democrats will no doubt argue also that such an implied repudiation of the President's policies will give aid and comfort to the enemy and weaken the President's voice in foreign affairs.

Because there is no way in which the voters can remove or force a resignation of the President himself, they will in effect be asked to support him with a Democratic Congress *whether or not they approve his domestic policies or his conduct of the war.* If the voters are convinced by this argument and do elect a Democratic majority for these reasons (perhaps even a larger Democratic majority than at present), the result is almost certain to be interpreted by the Administration as an endorsement of its domestic policies as well as of its conduct of the war. Here is a type of dilemma that occurs in some degree, indeed, in *any* mid-presidential-term Congressional election. It will occur in peculiar degree in November, 1942. Yet it is a dilemma that is caused solely by our constitutional provisions. It could not possibly arise under a parliamentary government.

To return to other of MacDonald's criticisms. During the President's fixed term of four years, MacDonald wrote, "he is practically beyond the reach of the people." The only way to remove him from office before his term expires is to impeach him; and impeachment is so cumbersome and grave a process that it has only once been attempted in our history, and then without success. Moreover, if impeachment is tried, it can only be for "treason, bribery, or other high crimes and misdemeanors." "Most of the things for which even the most unpopular Presidents have been criticized," MacDonald pointed out, following Wilson, "fall far outside the limits of this constitutional definition."

In short, "no change of opinion among the people and no amount of criticism in Congress can force any one out of office before the expiration of a fixed chronological term." The result is that the United States "has not a responsible government in any proper or effective sense. Political responsibility which must settle its accounts with the people only at fixed intervals of two, four, or six years, and settle even then in part only, is in practice not political responsibility at all." The inevitable tendency of our system has been "to widen the gulf between the government and the people, to discourage serious political thinking and debate save at moments of grave crisis, to increase the power of corrupt machine politics, and to cultivate an easy-going indifference to abuses. . . . The existing Constitution, however great its virtues in any particular respect, does not permit of genuine popular government. The rigidity of the electoral system, the divorce of the executive from the legislature, and the well-nigh uncontrollable power of the courts combine to centralize political power in the hands of a comparatively few individuals who are only remotely responsible to the people, and whose acts can be reviewed by the people only at long and fixed intervals."

Another American who raised his powerful voice for constitutional revision was Frank I. Cobb, the brilliant editor of the *New York World*. In an article in 1923,[1] Cobb called attention to the extraordinary fact that of all the self-governing nations that emerged from the blood and welter of the First World War, none fashioned its constitution after that of the United States. All of them rejected congressional government in favor of parliamentary government. Yet at that time the United States was at the zenith of its power and influence in international affairs. "No other country in all history had ever attained such prestige. . . . But none of the nations that owed its emancipation to American intervention in the war had sufficient admiration for the American political system to adopt it as the model for its own institutions."

It is not strange, Cobb continued, that the American people came to regard their Constitution as a fetish. For decades the government established under it was the only responsible expression of the principle

[1] "Is Our Democracy Stagnant?" *Harper's Magazine* (June, 1923). The article is reprinted in a volume compiled by JOHN L. HEATON, *Cobb of "The World"* (1924).

of free institutions to be found in a world of kings, emperors, autocrats and despots. But while other governments improved, ours remained stagnant. It is true that while exalting their Constitution the Americans were building up practices to supplement or even to circumvent the Constitution. They created the national convention, which, though without constitutional sanction or even ordinary legal authority, nonetheless took over the powers ostensibly held by the constitutional Electoral College and made the Electoral College a mere instrument to record the will of one of the two major party conventions.

Since Congress was "the outstanding failure of the Constitution," it was once thought that the sources of trouble lay in the election of Senators by the state legislatures, but when the Constitution was finally amended to provide for the election of Senators by a direct vote of the people, "nothing at all happened, except that the Senate declined rather than improved in ability." All that has come out of the direct primary, again, "is the disintegration of party government and the rise of bloc government, to the increasing dissatisfaction of the country."

Cobb shared the opinion of Bryce that our constitutional defects may have been the ultimate cause of the Civil War: "No sooner did a real issue become acute than the congressional system proved impotent to cope with it. Every other nation managed to rid itself of the institution of human slavery without violence. In the United States it was settled only by four years of civil war."

A NEW CONSTITUTION NOW

At the risk of wearying the reader by the repetition of arguments with which he has already grown familiar, it seems worth while to quote from the final paragraphs of Cobb's article, which sum up the case against our system:

The government of the United States cannot function at all in respect to policy when the President and a majority of Congress happen to belong to different parties. Neither can it function in respect to policy when the House and the Senate happen to be under different party control, which is by no means infrequent. The government can continue to perform the routine functions of administration, but for the rest it is deadlocked, until one side or another can win a decisive victory at the polls. When the victory is won, there is seldom general agreement in interpreting the meaning of the ballot —and there is always the Senate [only one-third of which can come up for any one election].

Whatever defects are inherent in parliamentary government, it has one unfailing source of strength. It must of necessity settle one thing at a time, and it is always possible to get a vote of the people on a single issue. What is equally important, responsibility cannot be evaded. There is no way of shifting it from the legislative to the executive department, and back from the executive to the legislative. There is no way of shifting it from the House to the Senate, or from the Senate to the House.

The American people were never before so critical of their government as they are now. They were never before so cynical about their government. They rail at the politicians, they jeer at Congress, they blackguard the

PRESIDENTIAL VS. CABINET GOVERNMENT

President, whoever he happens to be, but they never stop to inquire whether their government was established to meet the demands they are making on it. If they did, they would be obliged to admit that it was not. They ask a rigid, inflexible government to function as a responsive and flexible government. They ask a government of checks and balances to function as a political manifestation of democracy. They ask a government of co-ordinate and independent branches to function as a unit. It cannot be done. In spite of all their ardent devotion to the Constitution, it is apparent that they know little about the Constitution. They have turned it into a fetish and they burn a vast quantity of incense before it, but they have forgotten its origin and have lost contact with its purposes. What they think it is, or what they think it must be, is something that it was never intended to be, and can never be made to be, except by a process of almost revolutionary revision.

Has opinion regarding the merits and defects of the presidential system changed in the last twenty years among detached observers? Have our English friends, for example, had a change of mind regarding it since the days of Bagehot and Bryce? Such a change is not apparent. On the contrary, Englishmen whether of the Left or the Right are equally critical of the American system. Harold J. Laski, a declared Marxist, has in repeated volumes in the last two decades expressed his dislike of the presidential system and his decided preference for the parliamentary. Though his great admiration for the economic policies of Franklin Roosevelt has caused him to alter the opinion he expressed in 1925 that "the average American

President represents, at the best, a leap in the dark," [1] yet in *The American Presidency*, which appeared in 1940 and was almost a campaign document for Mr. Roosevelt, he still declared that "the case made, over seventy years ago, by Bagehot against the ultimate principles of the presidential system seems to me to have been strengthened, rather than weakened, by time." [2]

Mr. Laski himself made a powerful indictment of our political system in his volume *The Dangers of Obedience*, published in 1930:

If we assume that democratic government is desirable, there is hardly a canon of institutional adequacy against which the American system does not offend. It is desirable that the source of responsibility for governmental error or wrong should be clear and unmistakable; the American system so disperses responsibility that its detection is approximately impossible. It is urgent that the working of institutions should be conducted in the perspective of discussion which educates and clarifies the public mind; but the essential tasks of operation in America are almost wholly concealed from the public view. It is important that the occupants of high office should be chosen upon the basis of ability and experience; yet both the President and his Cabinet are selected by a process which, if it resembles anything, is akin to a dubious lottery. A governmental system, moreover, should be sensitive to the opinion of its constituents, and maximize the opportunity of translating a coherent body

---

[1] *A Grammar of Politics*, p. 300. Contrast this with the discussion in *The American Presidency*, pp. 50-53.
[2] *The American Presidency*, p. 248.

of doctrine into statute; yet it seems the purpose of American institutions deliberately to avoid the sensitiveness, on the one hand, and to prevent the making of coherent policy upon the other.[1]

Mr. Laski's criticism was written from the standpoint of the Left; but a generally conservative organ like the London *Economist,* though deeply dissatisfied with the average level of competence now to be found in Parliament, and recently suggesting reforms for it, is also convinced that the situation would not be bettered but only rendered much worse by the adoption of the American system: "A constitution in which the Executive is separated from the legislature is subject, at best, to deadlock, as so often in the United States, at worst, to dictatorship."[2]

5

I have cited the arguments of others, extending over three-quarters of a century, against the presidential system, because it has been my purpose to make clear that the weight of authoritative opinion has long advocated the constitutional revision here recommended. This proposal, in other words, is not being put forward merely to make our government more effective in the present crisis, vitally important as such an aim is, but to provide the form of government that would be most effective also in dealing with all normal political and economic problems. Yet with some readers this very marshaling of authorities may count

[1] *The Dangers of Obedience,* pp. 31-32.
[2] "The House of Commons," *The Economist* (Jan. 24, 1942), p. 96.

against me. If men have argued for this thoroughgoing revision for so many years, they may say, and nothing has been done, it must be because the country has considered their arguments and rejected them for good reasons.

There is no evidence whatever to support such a conclusion. The problem has never been brought before the American people in such a way as to force them to weigh the arguments for general constitutional revision or to think seriously about the matter at all. It has never seemed to the particular interest of any powerful organized group to do this. As each new crisis has arisen in our history, discussion has focused on the issues involved in that special crisis, to the neglect of the broader problem of the best *manner* of solving, of the best *political organization* for solving, that crisis and other crises. As the country drifted toward the Civil War, its attention was concentrated first on the issue of slavery and then on the issue of secession. But no one stopped to point out that it was our political machinery itself, with its opportunities for endless delays and obstruction by minorities, that made it impossible to settle minor problems and disputes as they arose but allowed these, rather, to accumulate and become a major problem and, finally, to become one that seemed soluble only by war.

If, even in the terrible ordeal that now confronts us, the nation cannot be brought to see the major role that our system of government itself plays in intensifying our difficulties and in creating many of them, and so in prolonging the war and increasing the sacri-

PRESIDENTIAL VS. CABINET GOVERNMENT

fices we must make, then we must develop a program to bring about this reform by gradual steps, and a technique to call constant attention to the necessity for such a reform. I shall have more to say about this program and technique in a later chapter.

III

SOME OBJECTIONS CONSIDERED

WHAT objections are likely to be raised to the adoption of responsible cabinet government in the United States? I do not have to speculate about these. A voluminous correspondence on the subject (some of it with leading Representatives, Senators, and other eminent American political figures) has given me a rather clear idea of them. Most of the objections I shall now consider are quoted, not invented, and I have tried to include every objection that has any plausibility at all.

There is no point in advocating cabinet government for America. The American people can never be persuaded to change their present form of government.

It is difficult to have much patience with this sort of objection. It is not an argument; it is simply the expression of a paralyzing fatalism. It helps to perpetuate the very condition it affects to deplore. The American people will compel a change to the cabinet form of government the moment they are actively convinced of the necessity for it. Those who are convinced that this change is imperative must try to persuade their fellow citizens.

Why imitate foreign systems? We want no slavish imitation of the English system.

The adoption of the essential principles embodied in the parliamentary system implies no "slavish imitation" of the political institutions peculiar to Great Britain. Certainly it is not necessary, for example, to emulate the British monarchy or the House of Lords: whatever desirable function either institution now performs could be much better performed by men not chosen on hereditary grounds.

The cabinet form of government, moreover, is not essentially "foreign." It is natural rather than contrived. It is the form of government adopted by practically all large American business corporations, by charitable and other public institutions, and by many labor unions. A board of directors or trustees or a central committee elected by the whole body concerned appoints the president, usually retaining the power to remove him if he is unwilling or unable to carry out their wishes. The president is the administrative head, makes periodic reports to the board, and adopts major policies or changes of policy only after obtaining its consent. The board corresponds to a parliament; its executive committee to a cabinet; the institution's president to a parliamentary premier. An American political institution that is the essential analogue of the parliamentary system is the city-manager form of government, now in existence in some 500 American towns and cities. Yet this form of government was not adopted through any conscious imitation of the parliamentary system; it was rather the outgrowth of a desire to run cities on "business principles."

As later chapters will make clear, the present writer favors innovations that would make our government far from an imitation of any foreign government. Serious objections would probably be based on the "experimental" nature of these proposals rather than on any "imitative" quality.

Why all this fuss about the mere machinery of government? What counts is the right MEN, *not the machinery. Our present wretched government is not the fault of our system but of our leadership.*

This sort of objection misses the point and begs practically the whole question at issue. It is something like saying: "What does it matter what kind of machine tools we put in our airplane-motor factories? All we want is large supplies of finely made and thoroughly dependable motors." Or, to take a somewhat closer analogy, it is like arguing: "What does it matter how our military forces are organized, as long as they can be counted on to make and execute the right tactical decisions?"

It is precisely the form of organization, of course, that may determine how the military forces do function. Political organization, like military, industrial or any other form of organization, does not exist merely for its own sake. It is not an end in itself but a means to an end. The very purpose of political organization should be to clarify and to educate the national will, and to discover, attract and put into power the leaders most capable of educating and effectuating that will. If "mere political machinery" is unimportant, then the very difference between a monarchy and a republic, or between dictatorship and democracy, is unimportant. For this resolves itself ultimately into a difference in political machinery. And differences of machinery can mean the difference between a good democracy and a bad one. Differences in machinery, in political institutions, can certainly mean an enormous difference in the quality of the leaders chosen and in the way they function. By effecting the *method* by which leaders are chosen, political machinery necessarily does a great deal to determine what *kind* of leaders are chosen.

Another form of the foregoing objection is: "It is not necessary to change our political machinery; it is merely necessary for Congress to consider bills more carefully." It is again "machinery," however—*i.e.*, the form of organization—that determines how carefully most bills are considered.

Still another and more subtle form of this objection is to disparage proposals for reforming political machinery by giving them some contemptuous name, like "gadgets." The London *Economist* questionably did this, for example, in an otherwise excellent article on the House of Commons in its issue of Jan. 24, 1942. I agree with the criticisms that *The Economist* proceeded to make of two of these "gadgets"—proportional representation and "functional" representation. I agree not because they are "gadgets" but because they are calculated to do more harm than good. *The Economist* then went on to advance some interesting proposals of its own, which it called, however, "simple proposals to make politics a *carrière ouverte aux talents*." But unsympathetic persons might call these "simple proposals" also "gadgets"—and so prevent consideration of them on their merits. There are plenty of complicated political schemes that would cause more trouble than they are worth. There are as many crackpot political as crackpot mechanical inventions. But real improvements are as possible, also, in the political as in the mechanical field. It is a very stupid conservatism that lumps all proposed political reforms under common condemnation.

Still a fourth form of this objection runs like this: "What difference does our 'organization' make? After all, the same American people will run the government in any case." This objection has already been answered. The methods of political selection determine the particular leaders selected. One form of political organization may educate, another may only atrophy the political acumen of a people. There is a broad sense, no doubt, in which every people controls its government. Even the decisions of a Hitler, Stalin or Mussolini are to some extent circumscribed and controlled by what the masses of his own people think. But the real questions are *how, when* and *by what methods* do the people control their government? How close, prompt and effective is their super-

SOME OBJECTIONS CONSIDERED

vision? Can they get rid of moderate evils as soon as they become aware of them? Or only of gross evils, and then only after a long lapse of time? The answer to these questions may determine the very survival of a country in a period of crisis when the time element is vital. Political reform, like military effort, can also be Too Little and Too Late.

Parliamentary government works well in England, because there are able men in the House of Commons, but the quality of men in Congress is so poor that there are no cabinet possibilities among them.

This is still another form of the objection just considered. It overlooks the effect of the particular kind of political organization itself in determining the quality of men that it attracts. As I shall later endeavor to show, there is no reason inherent in the cabinet system why the legislature *must* choose the premier or the cabinet from among its own members. It can seek a choice outside, just as the members of the great party nominating conventions commonly do in selecting a Presidential candidate. Certainly no one would say that even our present Congresses are inferior in political judgment to the delegates in the average nominating convention.

What is much more important, however, the objection overlooks the profound effect that the cabinet system itself, with the much more real possibilities it offers for recognition, responsibility and a great career in the legislature, would have in attracting abler men. Certain other reforms, such as the removal of the ill-advised residence requirement, which I shall later discuss, would also greatly raise the quality of Congress.

Political institutions and political organization are not important. They are in any case inevitably determined by economic forces. Economic forces are alone important. Class interests and the technical conditions of production inevitably determine the dominant economic and political opinions in any period, and consequently its legislation. Therefore tinkering with political machinery in the hope of securing substantially better government is futile.

In such a crude and extreme form this objection is untenable, yet in the last decade it has probably been one of the most influential of all arguments against the improvement of political institutions. Harold J. Laski, for example, most of whose writing has been about political principles and institutions, has seemed to devote himself in the last decade mainly to an attempt to demonstrate the futility of his own original preoccupation. In a series of volumes—*Democracy in Crisis* (1933), *The Rise of Liberalism* (1936), *Parliamentary Government in England* (1938), etc.—he has seemed to set himself with tedious emphasis to developing a thesis akin to this.

This thesis is the result of a slavish acceptance of Marxian dogmas that cannot bear serious examination. It embodies a whole chain of fallacious assumptions. It assumes for one thing that the masses of men act in accordance with their interests. Nothing could be more obviously untrue. If the masses of men acted in accordance with their real interests, would the world today be plunged in a savage war of destruction and mutual extermination? (To reply that a large percentage of these people have to "defend" themselves is to overlook the rest who are "attacking." By cold economic calculation, the people of the aggressor nations from the beginning stood to lose enormously more by their attempted conquests than they could ever hope to gain.)

Men do not act in accordance with their interests; they act in accordance with their illusions. To know what one's real interests are is an intellectual feat of which few men seem to be capable. "If all men acted from enlightened self-interest," as Bertrand Russell has put it, "the world would be a paradise in comparison with what it is." [1] There could be no greater disproof that men act with enlightened self-interest than the Marxists themselves, for they are blinded by hatred and envy—by what Bishop Butler called *disinterested malevolence*.[2] Butler was a far more profound student of human nature than Marx. If Marx had read the good bishop and profited by him, he would have saved himself from enormous fame and the world from enormous catastrophe.

The other assumption in this Marxist dogma is that men are guided not only by their own interests but merely by their own *economic* interests. At least their economic interests are supposed to be so predom-

[1] *Skeptical Essays* (1928), p. 53.
[2] *Sermons on Human Nature* (1726).

inant that no others have any important influence. Marx himself, if he had stopped to think about it, asked for no more income than enough to keep him working. If he was dominated by anything, it was the desire to improve the lot of the poor, or the desire to bring discomfiture to the rich, or the desire for fame as a writer. On any interpretation, he was dominated by *something else* than his own economic interest. He could have logically continued to hold on to his theory only by maintaining that he was himself merely one of the few negligible exceptions to his generalizations.

This assumption takes a further step. It assumes a *one-way chain of causation* in human affairs. It assumes that "technological conditions" determine class interests and the dominant economic opinions, and that the dominant economic opinions determine all other opinions and institutions. Now it is true that economic interests often determine economic opinions, and that economic opinions often determine political opinions. But the causation can also be the other way around. Political opinions often determine economic opinions. For example, a Southerner becomes a Democrat through geographic determinism: the New Dealers capture the Democratic party, and the Southerner, to continue to vote the Democratic ticket consistently, becomes a New Dealer. A man's economic opinions, moreover, often determine his conception of what his real economic interests are.

The Marxists always begin their reasoning at an

arbitrary point. They *take for granted* the "conditions of production" in any era, and fail to ask what forces, particularly what non-economic forces, may in turn have helped to bring about those conditions of production. Economic forces are indeed powerful. It is often convenient to try to study them in isolation, or to study their influence on other forces, or to make them the arbitrary starting points for the solution of specific problems. But it is quite another thing to turn this isolated study or this arbitrary starting point itself into a monistic or monoideistic philosophy.

If I may be permitted a personal confession at this point, let me say that my own main activity has been writing on economic, not political questions. But I have found myself forced more and more to turn to political questions as I have become more and more impressed with the futility of solving economic problems as long as political conditions are such as to make it impossible to *apply* correct economic solutions, even when they have been obtained. What we need are political techniques to ensure: (1) that genuine economic experts are consistently consulted regarding the solution of economic problems; (2) that their solutions and the arguments for them are properly publicized, so that the public may be instructed; and (3) that legislation shall be considered and drawn carefully enough, and with sufficient consultation of experts, to afford a reasonable hope that sound economic solutions of practical problems can be found and applied.

Political organization and institutions are of minor importance. What is important is the economic or other ideas that are prevalent in a nation. It is these ideas, in any case, which will be expressed in legislation and in government.

This is only another form of the objection just considered. But it is a much more reasonable one, and deserves separate consideration.

Let me say to begin with that I do not believe that good political institutions, by themselves, can bring a new heaven and a new earth. Good political institutions can do two things: they can instruct, and they can effectuate, the popular will. Good political institutions cannot in themselves guarantee that public opinion will be correct or benevolent. The popular will may itself be viciously mistaken. But if political institutions are of an instructive nature—if they provide for the consistent consultation of experts, for careful consideration of measures at various stages, for public debate by political leaders selected by a sound process, for concentration of responsibility—then the possibility that public opinion will be unhealthy on a given question will be substantially reduced.

Moreover, even though the good effects of good political institutions may seem limited, it would be hard to exaggerate the bad effect of bad political institutions. Bad political institutions may thwart the popular will altogether, and substitute for it the will of a self-seeking group or of a single megalomaniac. Or they may effectuate a mere caricature of the popu-

SOME OBJECTIONS CONSIDERED

lar will. Or, instead of instructing that will, they may be such as to pervert and degrade it.

Political institutions, in short, are not mere passive instruments for putting into effect popular economic and social ideas: they are themselves one of the chief determinants of such ideas.

The parliamentary system is suitable for countries like England, etc., but it cannot be used with a Federal system like ours.

I do not know why people say things like this. The disproof of the statement lies right next door to us, in Canada. Australia is another example of a federation of States with parliamentary government. Whether a country is or is not a federation of States is simply irrelevant to the respective merits of the presidential and the cabinet systems. A "federal" government, it is true, has more obvious need of a *written* constitution, prescribing and limiting its powers, than a government that has no separate States to consider. But this raises a wholly different question.

What advantage is there in adopting a parliamentary form of government? France had it, and it failed dismally.

This is the kind of objection that should interest students of semantics. It is the result of placing too much confidence in the mere *label* on an institution instead of examining the institution itself. Such labels —"parliamentary," "fascism," "democracy"—are a necessary form of shorthand for discussion, but they can be treacherous if they are used to conceal foggy concepts or as an excuse for ignoring the actual detailed workings of complex institutions.

The truth is that the now extinct Third Republic in France was not a parliamentary government but a travesty of parliamentary government. It was, in fact, almost deliberately designed to be so. The constitution was adopted by the National Assembly that ruled France from its election in February, 1871, until the end of 1875. A definitive government was delayed because a majority of the National Assembly were loath to recognize the republic proclaimed in Paris on Sept. 4, 1870, during the Franco-Prussian war. By postponing action they hoped to find a propitious moment for restoring a monarchy.[1] It was only because the monarchists were divided among themselves into mutually distrustful groups supporting Bourbon, Orleanist and Bonapartist candidates that a republic became at all possible. Even so, the complicated checks and balances introduced, and the failure to provide for a strong executive, suggest that an influential number of the framers were deliberately trying to create a form of republic that would break down and create a sentiment for the restoration of a monarchy. Those who hoped for this result did their work well. There were influential monarchist groups and organs until the day that the Third Republic fell. The Third Republic worked so badly that it produced—or at least increased—a corrosive distrust and cynicism

[1] *Cf.* BUEL W. PATCH, "Constitutional Reform in France" (1934), *Editorial Research Reports*, Washington, D. C.

SOME OBJECTIONS CONSIDERED

in France directed toward the whole political class.

The French Constitution of 1875 was modeled in some respects on the British Constitution and in some respects on our own. Unfortunately, it might be described as a mixture that combined the worst features of both the parliamentary and presidential systems and excluded the compensating virtues of either. It gave the French Parliament the power to force the resignation of the Premier and his Cabinet at any time. But it failed to do the only thing that could make the use of this power responsible and not merely capricious: it did not give the Premier the reciprocal power to force a dissolution of the Parliament. (Technically, the President had the power to dissolve the Chamber of Deputies with the consent of the Senate; but this consent proved so difficult to obtain that this technical right was never exercised after 1877.) This meant that the Deputies could force the resignation of the Premier for trivial reasons or for no reasons at all. For they could not be compelled to go back to the people to defend their action, and they could unseat the government without any risk to themselves. I have not compiled or seen an exact calculation of the final score; but a calculation in 1934 showed that the average duration of cabinets until that time had been eight months for the whole history of the Third Republic, five months for the period since the war and only three months during the two years preceding the calculation.[1] No strong or stable government was possible under such conditions.

[1] *Ibid.*, p. 240.

The power of dissolution in the hands of the premier, however, must force a recalcitrant parliament to think twice before it tries to unseat a cabinet. Such power in the hands of the premier makes the people, not the members of parliament, the final judges of a government. Under such conditions a parliament will vote to unseat a cabinet only if it is itself confident that its action will be supported by the voters. The result is that in England, the Prime Minister, instead of being a creature of a few months or sometimes days, as in France, has in the last century (1841-1942) had an average term of longer than three years. (That is, if each specific term of office is counted. But if we take instead merely the number of different individuals who have served one or more terms as Prime Minister in the period—which is the more important consideration so far as political experience and stable policy are concerned—then the average tenure of a Prime Minister in England in the last century rises to five and a half years. Some Prime Ministers have served terms as short as half a year; some have served uninterrupted terms as long as six or eight years; Gladstone, in four separated terms, served altogether more than twelve years. But this elasticity, enabling the country to drop quickly a Prime Minister who proves unfit or unpopular and to retain or re-choose one who shows preeminent fitness, is precisely what is desired.)

Another major error of the French Constitution is the same as one of our own. It created a bicameral legislature in which the second House had powers substantially equal to those of the first. It is impossible to achieve responsible parliamentary government under such a division of powers. The success of cabinet government depends upon the *fusion* of the legislative and executive powers. Our own Constitution not only breaks off the executive from the legislative power but breaks the legislative power itself in two —an arrangement calculated chiefly to provoke deadlocks, but at least self-consistent. The French Third Republic fused the executive power (what there was of it) to the legislative power, and then illogically sawed in half the legislative power itself. The result of such an arrangement was that though the Premier and Chamber of Deputies might agree on a measure, it could be blocked in the Senate. Obviously, under these circumstances, even if the Premier had had the power of dissolving the Chamber and forcing a new election, the election might have solved nothing; for though the new Chamber and Premier would have been brought into agreement by this device, the Senate might still fail to agree to a crucial program. The Senators were indirectly elected: one-fourth for life and the rest for overlapping terms of nine years. Even, however, if the French Constitution had granted the Premier the power to dissolve the Senate also, deadlock might still have existed after the election, if the country had elected (as the voters in our own States often do) a Chamber majority for one policy and a Senate majority for another. Recurrent deadlocks and paralysis of government must occur under any constitution that divides the essential legislative power.

A NEW CONSTITUTION NOW

These were the two main defects—and they were fatal defects—in the French Constitution. But on these were piled others, some only a little less serious. France adopted voting methods calculated to encourage the multiplication of parties. Its traditions also encouraged such multiplications. After the general election of May, 1932, the Chamber contained seventeen separate political groups. At the time of the French collapse there were at least ten such groups in the Chamber. The membership both of the Chamber and the Senate was absurdly excessive: the Senate had 314 members and the Chamber 618. The more membership of a legislature is multiplied beyond a reasonable point, the more clumsy and unmanageable it becomes, and the more its psychology approaches that of a mob.

It did not require the military defeat of 1940 to make these faults in the French Constitution clear. The majority of the French people, however faulty their individual analyses may have been of exactly what was wrong, were united in dissatisfaction with their political system. The Stavisky scandal finally precipitated the February riots of 1934 in Paris. Former Premier Tardieu declared at that time: "France . . . is a body without a head. And if one has seen a body without a head walking, one has always seen it fall in a few yards."[1] A contemporary account thus states the situation:

The next and fundamentally more important task of the Doumergue cabinet will be to attempt to bring

[1] "Reformer ou casser," *Revue des Deux Mondes* (Mar. 1, 1934).

about constitutional reforms designed to give France a more efficient governmental system. Until such changes are made, there can be little hope for permanent subsidence of the present political unrest. . . .

Thoughtful observers [recently] realized that existing conditions were producing a stalemate between the executive and the legislative branches of the government and that there was little scope for exercise of the strong leadership needed in a period like the present, so long as the executive was dominated to so great an extent by an intractable Chamber of Deputies. Hence there emerged a growing demand for constitutional reforms that would increase the powers of the executive, enable the government to act in emergencies with more decision and effectiveness, and free it from involuntary subservience to the will of a legislature elected for a long fixed term . . . where public opinion has no chance to assert itself directly except at stated intervals when there may be no paramount issues.[1]

I remarked a moment ago that it did not require the defeat of 1940 to make the faults of the French Constitution clear. It is possible to add that to a man of sufficient foresight no experience at all of that Constitution was needed to make its defects clear. At least one such man existed—Walter Bagehot. In a preface to the second edition of his *English Constitution*, which appeared in June, 1872, he discussed the provisional French Republic under Thiers, which had been in existence only about a year and a half. The Constitution of 1875 was yet to be adopted; but it followed in its main features the provisional struc-

[1] PATCH, *op. cit.*, pp. 240, 241, 248.

ture that had already been set up. Bagehot doubted that the new French Republic would be very successful. He began by pointing out that the experiment was being made "in a nation which has, to say the least of it, no peculiar aptitude for parliamentary government." (His judgment of America was the reverse of this.) "Every Assembly," he continued, "is divided into parties and into sections of parties, and in France each party, almost every section of a party, begins not to clamor but to scream . . . as soon as it hears anything which it particularly dislikes. With an assembly in this temper, real discussion is impossible, and parliamentary government is impossible too, because the parliament can neither choose men nor measures." The British Prime Minister, he added, "has the power of dissolving the assembly. But M. Thiers has no such power; and, therefore, under ordinary circumstances, I believe, the policy would soon become unmanageable. The result would be, as I have tried to explain, that the assembly would be always changing its ministry, that having no reason to fear the penalty which that change so often brings in England, they would be ready to make it once a month." [1]

Here is analytical foresight that touches clairvoyance. Bagehot could not have prophesied better had he been the seventh son of a seventh son.

Thus the French constitutional system proved fatally defective not because it was "parliamentary," but chiefly because it failed to grant the executive the powers essential to a parliamentary system. Like our

[1] World's Classics ed., pp. 296-297.

own system, also, unfortunately, it divided the legislative power in such a way as to produce deadlocks; and again like our own system, it allowed for a direct expression of public opinion at the polls only at rigidly fixed calendar intervals.

The parliamentary system was tried in Germany, with all the latest gadgets, and it broke down there.
Here again, as in the case of France, it is necessary to warn against placing too much confidence in the generalized *label* on an institution, which indicates a perhaps convenient but nonetheless arbitrary *classification*, instead of examining the merits of the specific institution itself. We must study the Weimar Constitution directly to determine what particular features caused it to work as it did. When we do so, we find in that constitution at least two special errors, to go no further, that caused it to work badly and, in the end, not at all.

One of these was the direct election of the President and the excessive powers given to the President. I speak here of one error and seem to mention two, but they were so closely connected as to constitute in effect one error. A government must have one, not two, executive heads. If the executive head of a parliamentary government is to be the premier (or "chancellor"), as he should be, then he should not also be the president. But if the president is directly elected by the people, and the premier is elected as such only indirectly by the parliament, the president will have, comparatively, excessive prestige and, what is worse, the wrong kind of prestige. He will regard himself as having a mandate from the people: he is almost sure to intervene unduly in the selection of premiers. In a parliamentary government the function of a president or a constitutional monarch is not to impose his own choice or judgment but to act, rather, as a sort of impersonal mirror to reflect or focus the will of parliament. The aged President Hindenburg used his own failing judgment and made the far from parliamentarily inescapable choice of Adolf Hitler.

The second great error of the German Constitution, even more harmful in its effects, was the adoption of proportional representation. This was the greatest single error, as well, of the Italian Constitution.

Let us consider Italy. It would be oversimplification to blame the fall of Italian democracy on any single cause. Yet the adoption of proportional representation was undoubtedly a very serious contributing cause. Now P.R., as it is called for short, has certain specious theoretical merits that have made it very attractive to many earnest social reformers; but it happens to have one glaring inherent defect that more than offsets all its attractions. By making it possible for all shades of opinion and all parties, no matter how small a section of the electorate they appeal to, to be represented in a legislature, it encourages a multiplicity of parties, it encourages extremists and extremisms of all sorts, and it discourages compromise or makes it impossible. Whatever may be said against the majority system, it has this great central merit:

it encourages the spirit of compromise; and the spirit of compromise, if it is not actually the heart of democracy, is absolutely essential to its successful continuance. The majority system usually brings about two main parties; and it forces those parties to think of their candidates and platforms in terms of their appeal to the community as a whole rather than to the party nucleus itself. P.R., on the other hand, is an instrument of disintegration. Instead of merely reflecting existing political divisions, it intensifies those that exist. What is essential in a democracy, if it is to act as a unit or to act effectively at all, is for all groups to focus upon the area of agreement among them. But the emphasis of P.R. tends to fall too heavily upon the area of disagreement.[1]

The Italian Chamber plunged for P.R. in 1919. As a result of the election by that system no single party had a majority in the new Chamber. Successive prime ministers found it impossible to govern. The Chamber was torn by strife between extremist groups; it contained Communists and Fascists who would have stood no chance of election under the old majority system. It was in this atmosphere, with the government's authority at low ebb, with civil war beginning to break out as a result, that the King turned to Mussolini, who, as is now well known, made his famous "march on Rome" in a sleeping car.

In the case of Germany, it is again important not to oversimplify, but it is no less important to stress

[1] *Cf.* F. A. HERMENS' pamphlet "Democracy and Proportional Representation."

the contributing role to Hitler's success played by P.R. As a result of P.R., it was impossible for any single party to get a majority of seats in the national assembly. In 1919, P.R. prevented the development of a Social-Democratic majority. In the years following, swarms of new parties were created, parties of extremists, and one of these was the National Socialist Party, which would have got practically nowhere under a majority system, under which parties would have had to appeal to moderate voters. The political history of Germany from 1920 on is the history of one great and permanent crisis—purposely made by the intrigues of minority groups. Minority cabinets had to beg for votes sometimes at the right and sometimes at the left, and thus were at the mercy of both. Dr. Bruening had to combine up to eleven groups in order to have his "majority of toleration." This created the atmosphere that made it possible for the Nazi extremists to work their way to power. They did everything possible to create the very division, bickering and ineffectiveness in democratic government to which they could point as a reason for getting rid of it.

It is unfortunate that space does not permit here a more adequate analysis of the manner in which P.R. made any workable and stable parliamentary government impossible in either Italy or Germany. The reader who is interested should consult either the short analysis by Prof. F. A. Hermens in his pamphlet "Democracy and Proportional Representation" or the much fuller analysis in the same writer's *Democracy or Anarchy?* Professor Hermens' analysis, to which the foregoing account is indebted, makes clear again and again the multiplication of parties and encouragement of extremists brought about by P.R. Under a majority system, he concludes, Mussolini's electoral chances "would have been exactly zero." In Germany he finds that "under a plurality system of voting the Social Democrats and Center Party combined would always have been sure of a large majority. Under such conditions there would have been little chance of success for Hitler."

As late as Apr. 5, 1942, a dispatch from Stockholm by George Axelsson, a correspondent of *The New York Times* who had recently been in Germany, remarked:

> The German inside today's Germany, even if he is capable of independent thinking, shudders at the thought of the thousand and one political parties of Weimar days, and out of this circumstance Hitler draws a good part of his present strength. . . . In the meantime, memory of what some Germans call "democracy at its worst," hampers the spread of democratic ideas and makes for loyalty to Hitler.

Earlier in this chapter I spoke of the fallacy of assuming that a people or its leaders counted for everything, and that their political organization was unimportant. It is now necessary to warn against the reverse error. We cannot assume that the organization is everything and that the people who are called upon to work it are of no particular importance. Obviously, a people and their political organization influence each other. This, in turn, does not mean that any organization that happens to exist among that people is "inevitable"; such fatalistic reasoning would lead to a Byzantine conservatism and a permanently frozen constitution. But it does mean that a political organization, no matter how theoretically ideal in itself, depends upon the people who operate it for its final efficiency. As John Stuart Mill has put it: "Political machinery does not act of itself. . . . In politics, as in mechanics, the power which is to keep the engine going must be sought for outside the machinery. . . . The people for whom the form of government is intended . . . must be willing and able to do what it requires of them to enable it to fulfill its purposes." [1]

We cannot blame a particular form of government, in brief, because a particular nation at a given time has not known how to use it. It would be nonsense to pretend that even the best contrived form of government could of itself bring the political millennium. Parliamentary government can merely enable public opinion to express itself most effectively both in quiet times and in times of crisis; but it cannot assure that the public opinion so expressed will always be a sensible or a healthy one. On the other hand, this is no ground for arguing that the form of political organization does not matter, or that it is of no importance

[1] The whole discussion by Mill of the relations of a people to their governmental organization, in the first chapter of his *Representative Government*, To What Extent Forms of Government Are a Matter of Choice, is distinguished by its rare sense and balance.

whether a nation allows itself to be encumbered, or its will actually sidetracked or perverted, by bad political machinery. Just as neither heredity nor environment can by itself fully explain an individual, so neither a people's "natural" qualities nor their political organization can of itself account for their political decisions. We must consider both, in their complex interdependence.

After we have examined, therefore, any particular constitution to determine the good or bad effects of this or that clause or institution, we must attempt to separate from these the merits or defects in the temper or traditions of the nation working that constitution. The Weimar Republic, there can be no doubt, collapsed partly through the defects of its Constitution and partly through deep-seated undemocratic traditions in Germany and an unhealthy state of public opinion.

IV

MORE OBJECTIONS

IF WE are to examine, as I promised in the last chapter, every argument against cabinet government for America that seems even plausible, we must still deal with a number of objections.

Parliamentary government may be all very well for the English, but we are a temperamentally unstable people, and with us it would only lead to frequent and violent changes in the government, as with the French.

There are several misconceptions here, which need to be dealt with separately. It is true, as we have just seen, that the temperament and traditions of a people determine how they will work a given constitution. But as we have also seen, the French comparison here is fallacious. Whatever may have been the defects of the French political temperament, the instability of their governments under the Third Republic was mainly owing to cardinal defects in their Constitution. Bagehot, who recognized the defects in the French political temper even before the Constitution of 1875 was adopted, recognized at the same time that the inability of the Premier to dissolve a refractory

Parliament was a more serious cause for misgivings.

A few pages back I pointed out that as against the average tenure of only a few months for a French Premier, the average uninterrupted term of a British Prime Minister was longer than three years, and his average total tenure five and a half years. This long tenure under parliamentary government is not peculiar to Great Britain. Few persons would say that our Canadian neighbors are more stable in temperament than we are. Yet the record since 1867 shows that the average uninterrupted term of a Premier there has been more than five years, and his average total tenure more than seven years. The present Canadian Prime Minister, Mr. Mackenzie King, has now served three terms over a total of fifteen years. When the Premier has the power of dissolution, the alleged instability of parliamentary government is found to be a myth.

The belief of Americans that they are emotionally unstable and must protect themselves against their own future states of mind is a very curious phenomenon. One of the most instructive examples of the effects of this self-distrust was the neutrality acts of 1935, 1936 and 1937, and the modification of 1939. Congress first provided that articles of war could not be sold to a nation at war, and then that they could be sold only if the purchaser would pay cash in full and carry the goods in his own ships. These provisions were enacted not primarily to ensure that the American exporter would get paid or that American lives would not be lost by submarine sinkings; they were enacted for fear of what our own emotional response would be if American ships were sunk and American lives lost. We did not trust ourselves to decide a future situation upon its merits. The Neutrality Act assumed that we could make a better decision about a future state of affairs before we knew what that future state of affairs was going to be than we could after we did know it. It was an attempt to protect ourselves against our own future knowledge. The result, when the new situation arose, was merely to hamstring our capacity for appropriate action and to cause needless and harmful delays.

Still another illustration of our effort to protect ourselves against our own future decisions is the legal national-debt limit—a symbolic restriction that Congress is constantly imposing on its future actions and constantly having to change.

This strange form of national self-distrust, in fact, lies at the base of our excessive checks and balances. We provide constitutionally that no Congressman shall be elected who is not at the time of his election an inhabitant of the State from which he is chosen. We do this for fear that the actual people of that State may sometimes prefer to be represented by persons who are not inhabitants of the State. To natural local prejudices we add a purely artificial restriction. Yet we are surprised and indignant when Congressmen think habitually only of their own States and districts and neglect the welfare of the nation as a whole. We are constantly trying to protect ourselves in advance against what we may think of and do about a future situation when it arrives and we actually know what it is. In a whole network of constitutional restrictions, traditions and laws, the American people or their representatives assume their own prescience at the time that they impose the restrictions and their own future incompetence. In brief, we impose our self-restrictions in the mood of an inordinately self-confident father drawing up the conditions of a will for what he assumes is to be a certainly irresponsible and possibly idiotic son. We do not even have his excuse, because we are both father and son.

When Americans object that we are too unstable a people for parliamentary government, they supply but another illustration of this mood. This objection postulates that, if we allow ourselves to change our governmental leaders whenever we have lost confidence in their desire or ability to carry out our wishes, then we shall lose confidence too often; we shall be capricious; we shall listen to sophists and demagogues; we shall throw out governments that know better what is good for us than we do. The answer to this sort of objection is that if we are really as bad as all that, it is difficult to see what protection is afforded by our present inflexible checks-and-balances government. If we are likely to throw out the right leaders and put in the wrong leaders in a crisis, or on a particular concrete issue, what prevents us from doing so whenever an election is held? In brief, if we are mercurial, irresponsible, and capricious by nature, then we are just as likely to be so on the first Tuesday after the first Monday in November every two or four years as on any day of any year. If we are incompetent to choose or change our own leaders at will, then we are incompetent to choose or change them at intervals rigidly fixed in advance. The rigid election intervals, someone may say, will at least protect us from acts of national folly in between. But suppose that the last election was itself an act of national folly? Then our rigid system forces us to suffer the consequences of our folly for four years—a time period that may be disastrous—even though the majority have long recognized their mistake and wish to correct it. Nobody denies that the American people are fallible. But they should have the same political opportunity that the English people have, and that each American enjoys as an individual in the conduct of most of his own affairs—the opportunity of correcting a mistake as soon as its consequences have become apparent.

Have the American people, in fact, the political incompetence assumed by the objection to parliamentary government that we are now discussing? Certainly not in the judgment of most impartial observers. There was never a shrewder political judge than Walter Bagehot. Seventy-five years ago, he wrote:

> The Americans now extol their institutions, and so defraud themselves of their due praise. But if they had not a genius for politics; if they had not a moderation in action singularly curious where superficial speech is

so violent; if they had not a regard for law, such as no great people have yet evinced, and infinitely surpassing ours—the multiplicity of authorities in the American Constitution would long ago have brought it to a bad end. Sensible shareholders, I have heard a shrewd attorney say, can work *any* deed of settlement; and so the men of Massachusetts could, I believe, work *any* Constitution.[1]

Why change our own stable form of government for the unstable parliamentary form?

This is in some respects only another form of the previous objection. It involves an ambiguity in the meaning and application of "stable" and "unstable." It uses the word "stable" when it means rigid, and "unstable" when it means merely flexible. It tends to confuse also the stability of *the jobs of the holders of public office,* in which only the officeholders themselves need be directly interested, with the stability of the *nation,* in which we should all be primarily interested. But as we have seen, it does no good but only great harm if we attempt to make the tenure of the holders of office outlast the confidence of the people in those officeholders. A government should continue just as long as the people of the country have confidence in it, and no longer.

It is true that we do not want changes of government for trivial or frivolous reasons. But a parliamentary government may be made just as stable in this respect as desired. I shall later discuss possible devices by which this flexible stability can be achieved.

[1] *The English Constitution,* p. 202.

The parliamentary system has the great defect that the executive must resign even if defeated on a single measure.

This objection rests on a misunderstanding of how the parliamentary system really works. It implies that a premier may be overthrown through purely accidental, irrelevant or trivial reasons. In a soundly designed parliamentary system, however, this is in the highest degree improbable. Under such a system a parliament is always aware of the gravity of its vote. It knows in advance that its vote on a particular government measure, even a measure apparently unimportant in itself, might force the resignation of a ministry. Therefore it will not vote against that measure unless it actually *wishes* the resignation of the ministry. And if the premier has the power of dissolving the parliament, as he should have, the members will have a far stronger reason for not voting against the measure: they will not wish to end their own terms of office and be forced to run for election again. This will be particularly true if the premier is known to be popular, for then they will feel that their chances of winning against him are slight. Unless the parliament actually passes a direct vote of lack of confidence in the government, moreover, it is for the premier to decide whether or not he shall resign, or threaten to resign, on the defeat of any single measure.

It is easy to devise, as I shall later show, at least a "forty-eight hour veto," under which the premier could force a second vote on any bill if he thought that its defeat had been merely accidental. But this is essentially a secondary device. For it should be clear, when one considers the matter, that although the defeat of a single measure (unless it is a crucial one) may sometimes be the *pretext* for overthrowing a "government" under the parliamentary system, it is almost never the real cause. The real cause is basically loss of parliament's confidence in the "government" itself, supplemented by its belief that the country has also lost confidence in the "government." Under such circumstances the cabinet *ought* to fall; or there should at least be a new election in the country to determine what the people's sentiment really is. There is nothing merely accidental or trivial in such a forced resignation of the government. It is far less accidental in any real sense than an election imposed on the country for no better reason than that a specified calendar date has rolled round.

Our presidential form of government is needed because a President must be assured in advance of time to carry out his legislative program.

It is necessary to untangle the various assumptions implicit in this objection. Insofar as it is sound, it seems to me an argument for the parliamentary rather than for the presidential form of government. If there is an elaborate long-time legislative program, it is much more desirable to have it the program of a party than that of a single individual. A party program is a result of the democratic process of consultation and compromise and not the result of personal whim or caprice.

There is, again, no necessary relationship between a legislative program and a four-year term or series of four-year terms. I cannot recall any instance in American history in which a President came into power pledged to carry out any elaborate legislative program, requiring a long time for passage, the essential outlines of which he had previously revealed to the voters. At best, the presidential candidates debate one leading proposal, which can usually be put into effect by a single bill. For the rest, they deal with circumstances as they arise or propose particular measures as such measures occur to them. I cannot think of any self-consistent program that requires years to put into effect unless it is a program of gradualist socialism.

But there is certainly no peculiar connection between a long-range legislative program and the presidential system. On the contrary, by the division of the executive from the legislature under that system, the legislature may be from the beginning opposed to the President's program. If originally in agreement, it may be changed to an opposing House by the mid-term elections. A legislative "program," again, may require six months, one year, five years or six years; there is certainly no reason for assuming any necessary correspondence with a term of four years. Nor is there any argument for permitting an administration to go ahead with a program when the people have lost confidence in that program or may be sharply opposed to it. The parliamentary form permits a government to stay in power just as long as its legislative program is approved by the country, and no longer.

We do not want a chief executive who is forced to be subservient to the legislature.
This objection would apply to the French system under the Third Republic, but hardly to a system, as in England, where the executive has power to dissolve the legislature if it opposes him.[1] On the contrary, under such a system the executive has much more power over the legislature than in our own, where the President can often exert influence only by the obnoxious practice of patronage.

The delays forced by our Constitution are not a liability but an asset. They compel us to give careful consideration to proposed changes.
A nation can erect a complicated set of hurdles and barriers to compel itself to delay decisions, but it cannot thereby compel itself to think correctly, or even carefully, about a decision. By the obstacles it erects, it discourages itself from making *any* new decision, regardless of its merits. The self-erected barriers tend to bias its decision unduly against the proposed change. "The process of amending the [American] Constitution," wrote Bryce, "is so troublesome that even a change which involves no party issues

---

[1] Nominally, the King dissolves Parliament in England, but only at the Prime Minister's direction.

may remain unadopted long after the best opinion has become unanimous in its favor." [1]

But another result is to lead to short cuts—*i.e.*, to attempts to circumvent the plain meaning of the Constitution. As Bagehot wrote seventy years ago:

> Every alteration [of the American Constitution], however urgent or however trifling, must be sanctioned by a complicated proportion of States or legislatures. The consequence is that the most obvious evils cannot be quickly remedied; that the most absurd fictions must be framed to evade the plain sense of mischievous clauses; that a clumsy working and curious technicality mark the politics of a rough-and-ready people. The practical arguments and the legal disquisitions in America are often like those of trustees carrying out a misdrawn will—the sense of what they mean is good, but it can never be worked out fully or defended simply, so hampered is it by the old words of an old testament.[2]

Congress would be more subject to pressure groups than it is now if we had a parliamentary form of government.

The argument in this case is that if Congressmen could be voted out of office at any time that the premier called a general election on a particular issue, they would be far more likely, even than now, to yield to pressure from special interests and groups. The experience of Great Britain, however, has not shown this to be true. Neither, for that matter, has the example of our own House compared with our

---
[1] *The American Commonwealth* (1914 ed.), Vol. I, p. 215.
[2] *The English Constitution*, p. 199.

MORE OBJECTIONS

Senate. Though our House is elected every two years and our Senate for overlapping terms of six years, it is the Senate that has been more subservient to such lobbies as those of the farm bloc, the veterans, the silver interests and the labor unions.

This is probably not accidental. The reason may be uncovered in a dictum of Senator Elihu Root to the effect that "majorities often forget, but organized minorities always remember." What he meant was this: if the members of an organized minority group want some special favor, such as a subsidy from the treasury, the granting or withholding of that favor will make such a profound difference to their special interests that they will never forget, even after years, how their Congressmen voted on the question. The granting of the subsidy or other favor, though at the expense of the entire country, will, on the other hand, make so little direct difference to the welfare of any individual voter not in the group, and that difference will often be so difficult to trace, that he will quickly forget the cowardice of his Congressmen for yielding to the demand of the special interest or their courage in resisting it. Thus it is not difficult to see why the interested groups have memories so much longer than the relatively disinterested majority. But the result may be very different if the "general" voter has the potential opportunity to vote upon the issue immediately. There will then be enough voters recognizing the merits of the issue, to prevent the intimidation of the Congressman by the votes of the interested minority.

There is another and more important factor to be considered. In cabinet government the executive must take a position on all questions, on all bills or amendments, however minor. The British Prime Minister cannot "pass the buck" to Parliament on an embarrassing issue, a "hot potato," as the President can to Congress. A measure is either a "government measure" or it is not: the premier must take his stand. It need hardly be said that in his own interests he will have to be above mere local or petty considerations. His position will also give courage to members of his party, who can vote on the question as a "government measure" rather than on their mere personal responsibility. Finally, a good cabinet government would adopt the wholesome rule of the British system, under which no expenditure can be proposed except by the government. This alone would be sufficient to protect the private member against most pressure groups.

Legislators under cabinet government, in brief, are far better protected against pressure groups than under presidential government. They can act as a body, under disciplined party responsibility, and not as mere lonely and exposed individuals. Several other changes, moreover, could easily increase their independence. If our Constitution were altered, for example, to permit a particular Representative or Senator to be elected from any State or district, it would make Congressmen far more independent of local interests and pressure than they are now.

Why is it necessary to institute parliamentary government to get our representatives to respond to public sentiment? Do not the President and Congress already do so now?

This objection is plausible because it embodies a half-truth. It is true that the President and Congress often respond in a rough way to public sentiment and even to changes in public sentiment. But in any particular case the real question concerns what sort of response is made. Let us take as an example the Supreme Court enlargement issue raised by Franklin D. Roosevelt early in 1937. If the Gallup poll is to be taken as a reliable indication, the President's proposal was unpopular from the start. There was a narrow majority against it in the country as soon as it was made, and this majority increased in the next few months as the public debate on the issue proceeded. Certainly the majority in Congress was against the proposal, in spite of party discipline and the President's prestige, just recently increased by his reelection. The proposal, it is true, was finally defeated. But if we had had parliamentary government, this disturbing proposal would almost certainly not have been made. If it had been made, the President would have had to resign as a result of its defeat.

Before springing this proposal upon the country, the President had not even consulted his own party leaders in Congress, who were as much taken by surprise as anyone else. This would not have been possible under cabinet government, in which the leading proposals are party proposals, the result of group decision, and not the result of the whim of a single man. It is obvious why this must be so: the prime minister depends for the very tenure of his office on the constant support of the other leaders of his party, particularly in parliament; the President, at most, needs that support for his tenure of office for only the few months of his election campaign. Though the President had never mentioned his Supreme Court proposal throughout his reelection campaign a few months before, he kept insisting that he had a "mandate" from the people to introduce this reform. Under the presidential system there was no definite way of settling this particular point. But under a parliamentary system it could have been settled very promptly and emphatically. If the proposal had been made and Congress had rejected it, the Chief Executive could have dissolved Congress and appealed to the country. A vote then and there on the candidates supporting and opposing the proposal would have definitely answered the question whether or not the President had a mandate for that particular scheme.

But, it will be argued, did not precisely that test eventually come? Did not the President run for office in 1940? Was not a new Congress elected in that year, as well as in 1938? And was not the Supreme Court proposal one of the factors that the voters were able to take into consideration in the judgment they then rendered? These questions, however, precisely illustrate the difficulties that our presidential form of government creates. In the 1938 elections, in spite of the attempted Presidential "purge," the overwhelming majority of the opponents of the President's court plan were reelected. When the next presidential election day finally rolled round, nearly four years had passed since the Supreme Court issue had been raised. It had meanwhile been all but forgotten. It seemed insignificant beside the issues that had since arisen, particularly concerning America's relationship to the European war. Mr. Roosevelt did not raise the Supreme Court issue in 1940. His opponent, as I recall, made one or two parenthetical references to it, but never presented it effectively or even devoted a single important speech to it. What role did the issue actually play? Clearly this crude, uncertain and dilatory method of reflecting public sentiment is not to be compared with the parliamentary method, which permits a test of public sentiment on a specific issue at the precise time when that issue is to be decided. To test public sentiment by a vote that may not come until years *after* an issue has been decided (and after many subsequent issues have been raised) is academic at best. In certain circumstances such a delay can even prove disastrous.

There is another question involved here. It is frequently and solemnly insisted that the American people should vote on "issues," not "men." It is a maxim, however, that no one dreams of following in his private affairs. When directors choose the president of a corporation, when, in fact, anyone is hired in private life in any capacity, the choice is determined only in minor degree by the specific answers that the applicant gives regarding his views on the "policies" that should be followed. The choice is based primarily on the employer's view of the applicant's general competence—on not merely his declared willingness but his actual ability to carry out whatever "policies" may be decided upon. The main question, in brief, is not the applicant's announced "policies" but—does he measure up to the job?

This is, or should be, also the main question to be asked of a public official. In the midst of a great war the voters are not competent to pass upon the specific strategy of the war or the huge maze of organizational questions that it raises. The voters cannot be expected to choose between Strategic Plan X or Strategic Plan Y. They cannot be expected to decide whether there should be a unified board of strategy or a separate air force; whether our troops or "lease-lend" aid should be scattered over a score of points or concentrated on a single decisive front; or what specific taxation, labor or industrial policies should be followed. But they are competent to decide whether the conduct of the war is in the right hands; whether their existing leaders are or are not those most likely to conduct the war to a successful conclusion. The British people have the means to make this decision. The American people have not. The British people had the legal means, which they exercised, to remove Mr. Chamberlain at the very height of their gravest crisis and to try Winston Churchill in his place. They have the legal means, in turn, to change Mr. Churchill for someone else if he fails to measure up to their hopes. The American people do not have the legal means of removing their own war leader, no matter how fatally poor an administrator or director he may prove to be. Whether the President or Congress is "forced to yield to public sentiment" on a specific point, therefore, may be very unimportant. The really important decision—that of a change in existing leadership itself when it proves incompetent to carry out the national will—is one which the American public is powerless to make.

One result of this impotence of the people to make their opinions effective, as we have seen, is to pervert the nature of the opinions themselves. There is a pathology of masses as well as of individuals. When an individual feels powerless to correct a certain situation in his private life, he often refuses to face the situation realistically. He argues to himself that the situation is not so bad as it seems. In the same way, when the American people are powerless legally to change their leaders, above all during a war, many of them will refuse to face the full truth about their leaders. Fearing that vigorous criticism will only divide the country without bringing about the changes necessary, they deliberately tone down their criticism or confine it to this or that special minor point, on which they hope that reform may be possible. But if the leaders are truly incompetent for their task, the issue of their fundamental incompetence will never be squarely raised. The leaders of thought themselves may refuse to draw this conclusion even privately, because they feel that even if the conclusion is correct, *nothing can be done about it.*

Can we not get the reforms necessary—or at least a substantial part of them—without taking so radical a step as changing our Constitution? For example, can we not achieve much of the advantage of the British system merely by forcing the President to submit to questioning in Congress? Could we not achieve a great improvement if only the Senate were to change its rules of debate to make the filibuster impossible? Would not a great step forward be possible if Congress merely consented to change its internal organization, choosing a central committee on legislation, let us say, instead of some eighty different competing committees?

A large number of questions are raised here, but it is convenient to consider them together. This sort of objection fails to recognize that unless fundamental constitutional changes are made, these minor reforms are themselves usually either undesirable or close to impossible.

What would be the point, for example, of simply forcing the President (even if it is assumed that this could be done without a constitutional amendment) to submit to questioning in Congress? If the President's policies were such that his answers to Congress were always satisfactory, the practice would be needless. But suppose that the President's answers were unsatisfactory to Congress? What could be done about it that cannot be done already? Certainly Congress would perform no public service if it were able to "show up" the President in this way. For though this would undermine public confidence in the President, there would be no way of changing him—hardly a desirable situation. On the other hand, if the President consistently got the better of the clash of wits, it would not help him much with his legislative program. He could not force a change of Congress. The institution of questioning the President in Congress would be valuable only in conjunction with the right of Congress to force a resignation or of the executive to force a dissolution.

It seems to me, again, that the iniquity of the Senate rules of debate has been greatly exaggerated. Ordinarily, it is true, Senators are privileged to talk interminably, and to wander from the question before the Senate as much as they please. It could be argued, however, that on net balance the Senate debating rules have achieved as much good as harm. Certainly the opinion of each of us is greatly influenced by the particular measure that the Senate is delaying. If the Senate chronically debates too much, moreover, it is compensating for a House that chronically, and especially of late years, debates far too little. We must remember, also, that the Senate has a rule for bringing debate virtually to a close that can be invoked upon the approval of two-thirds of the Senators present. I should like to see this supplemented by a rule that would restrict debate on a given measure, though less severely, upon approval of a mere majority of Senators present. But I think the importance of this question has been overstressed by persons who are eager to get some favorite measure passed, or who despair of seeing more thoroughgoing constitutional changes achieved.

To change the internal organization of Congress, it is true, would be a reform of real importance, and one that could in theory be achieved without any change in the Constitution. It would be a great forward step if, instead of having some eighty standing committees in Congress as at present (forty-seven in the House and thirty-three in the Senate), each with the power to introduce or smother legislation, there were one central committee (analogous to the British Cabinet) with this power. I shall later devote a special chapter to this reform. But here it is important to point out that formidable forces of tradition, individual prerogative and vested interest stand in the way. The proposal for change will certainly not come from the existing heads of the multitude of permanent committees in Congress. These heads of committees have come to their positions not on their merits as recognized by their present fellow members but by the rule of seniority. They are "sitting pretty," and mean to hold on to their prerogatives and power. The situation is not likely to be challenged, either, by the majority members next in line under the seniority rule, or by the ranking minority members of the committees, who stand to be the actual heads if there is a shift in the balance of parties in Congress. Why, then, does not the new member, the "outsider," the man who has got poor committee assignments, challenge the arrangement? Because, unless his campaign can be assured of success in advance, no individual member wants "to stick his neck out" by incurring the displeasure of the existing Congressional leaders and committee heads, who have it in their power to decide whether or not he shall get a good appointment and be an influential member of Congress. It may be almost as difficult to effect this change, in short, as it would be to amend the Constitution directly.

The proposal for a change to parliamentary government may have great merit, but it should be considered only in some quiet time, when we can think calmly and objectively about the matter. When the country is fighting for its very existence, it should not be diverted by the consideration of a disrupting reform of this kind.

This kind of objection to a proposal was satirized more than a century ago by Jeremy Bentham in his *Book of Fallacies*. I quote, since it is more easily available, from the contemporary condensation of Bentham's satire by Sydney Smith:

Procrastinator's Argument.—"Wait a little, this is not the time."
This is the common argument of men, who, being in reality hostile to a measure, are ashamed or afraid of appearing to be so. [Not] *today* is the plea—*eternal exclusion* commonly the object. . . . There is in the minds of many feeble friends to virtue and improvement, an imaginary period for the removal of evils, which it would certainly be worth while to wait for, if there was the smallest chance of its ever arriving—a period of un-

exampled peace and prosperity, when a patriotic king and an enlightened mob united their ardent efforts for the amelioration of human affairs. . . . These are the periods when fair-weather philosophers are willing to venture out, and hazard a little for the general good. But the history of human nature is so contrary to all this, that almost all improvements are made after the bitterest resistance, and in the midst of tumults and civil violence —the worst period at which they can be made, compared to which any period is eligible, and should be seized hold of by the friends of salutary reform.[1]

To this I am tempted to add also a quotation from Macaulay's speech on parliamentary reform of Dec. 16, 1831:

What then, it is said, would you legislate in haste? Would you legislate in times of great excitement concerning matters of such deep concern? Yes, Sir, I would; and if any bad consequences should follow from the haste and the excitement, let those be held answerable who, when there was no need of haste, when there existed no excitement, refused to listen to any project of reform, nay, who made it an argument against reform, that the public mind was not excited. When few meetings were held, when few petitions were sent up to us, these politicians said, "Would you alter a constitution with which the people are perfectly satisfied?" And now, when the kingdom from one end to the other is convulsed by the question of reform, we hear it said by the very same persons, "Would you alter the representa-

---

[1] *The Letters of Peter Plymley* (1929 ed.), pp. 106-107. In Bentham's *Book of Fallacies* (1824)—alas, out of print—the "Fallacies of Delay" are grouped in Part III.

tive system in such agitated times as these?" Half the logic of misgovernment lies in this one sophistical dilemma: If the people are turbulent, they are unfit for liberty: if they are quiet, they do not want liberty.

I allow that hasty legislation is an evil. I allow that there are great objections to legislating in troubled times. But reformers are compelled to legislate fast, because bigots will not legislate early. Reformers are compelled to legislate in times of excitement, because bigots will not legislate in times of tranquillity. If, ten years ago, nay, if only two years ago, there had been at the head of affairs men who understood the signs of the times and the temper of the nation, we should not have been forced to hurry now. If we cannot take our time, it is because we have to make up for their lost time. If they had reformed gradually, we might have reformed gradually; but we are compelled to move fast, because they would not move at all.[1]

I do not wish to imply, by these quotations, that most of those who raise this objection against reforming now are insincere. On the contrary, they undoubtedly raise it in perfect sincerity and good faith. But there is both a general and a specific answer to it. The general answer is that to put off a proposed reform from a disturbed time to a "quiet" time is to put it off indefinitely; for if the quiet time actually arrives, people tend to reverse their positions and argue that there is no real urgency for so sweeping a reform when things are going along well. This brings us to our specific answer.

[1] *Speeches on Politics and Literature* (Everyman ed.), pp. 53-54.

Since its adoption 153 years ago, we have not fundamentally revised our Constitution. Yet all but a very few years in this century and a half have been years of peace. In "quiet" times the issue of basic constitutional revision seems academic. Harold J. Laski, in his volume *The Dangers of Obedience,* complained in 1930 of precisely this situation. Necessary as drastic revision of the American Constitution was, he wrote at that time, the prospect of achieving it was still remote, "if only because, in a period of calm, people can rarely be persuaded to prepare themselves for times of storm." In Bryce's phrase, the defects of our Constitution in such times seem merely a "teasing ailment." But it is precisely in a time like the present, as Bryce prophetically warned, that the defects of the Constitution could become a "mortal disease."

Revising the Constitution is *not* a "diversion" from the war effort, any more than a reform of military organization or personnel at such a time is a diversion from the war effort. It is, on the contrary, one of the most essential things we must now do to organize our government properly to conduct a war. If we win without such a reform, we may be sure that it will be only at a greater cost in domestic disruption, and at a far greater sacrifice of time and lives and treasure, than would otherwise have been necessary. So narrow is the margin in this tremendous conflict that failure to adopt such a reform might, indeed, make the difference between victory and defeat.

It is too late to revise the Constitution. Our constitutional democracy is dying, and under the forces let loose by the war, we are being swept willy-nilly into a form of left-wing totalitarianism. The Constitution will not be amended; it will simply be forgotten. Or, at best, it will be "interpreted," without effective resistance, to give the holders of office whatever powers they may wish to usurp.

The argument that it is too late to revise our Constitution cannot, of course, be consistently made by the same persons who contend that it is too early. But each argument must be dealt with on its own merits.

To assert that it is too late to revise the Constitution is simply a form of fatalism and defeatism. We can avoid Fascism in America, of the Left or Right, just as long as enough of us are vigilant to do so. The better our democracy works, the greater the number of its defenders will be; the worse it works, the fewer will be those eager to preserve it. Therefore, to prevent catastrophic changes, we should put into effect while there is still time the reforms in our constitutional machinery that common sense and experience show to be necessary. As W. Y. Elliott, pointing to historic precedent, has warned: "It is not those who would reform but those who would ossify a constitution who bring about its destruction." [1]

[1] W. Y. Elliott, *The Need for Constitutional Reform* (1935), p. 207.

V

TOWARD THE CABINET SYSTEM

IN THIS chapter we shall consider the minimum changes that would be necessary to give America a genuinely flexible and responsible democratic government. In the following three chapters we shall inquire what political institutions would be most desirable in themselves if we were starting, so to speak, with a clean slate, and did not have to take into account the vested interests, customs and habits of thought that inevitably stand in the way of reform. The latter inquiry, I hope, will not be regarded as too hypothetical or academic. It is only by trying to formulate our ultimate ideals, sometimes even in detail, that we can make sure that our minds are clear on a subject. At the very least, such an inquiry is necessary if we are to assure ourselves that the immediate reforms we do adopt are those calculated to take us in the right direction.

The first need of a genuinely responsible democratic government, as we have seen, is the fusion of the executive and the legislature, instead of their separation, and consequent always latent antagonism, as in our existing presidential system. Our system gives rise both to chronic deadlocks and to irresponsibility.

TOWARD THE CABINET SYSTEM

Because the legislature can thwart the will of the President or the President can veto the will of the legislature (unless that will is almost unanimous), and because one House of our legislature can veto absolutely the will, no matter how overwhelming, of the other House, action of the greatest urgency is often not taken at all. And the public is unable to see precisely who is responsible either for failure to act or for the adoption of some shabby compromise that everybody is eager to disown.

This inherently almost unworkable system is made to work at all only by the abandonment in practice by one agency or the other of its theoretical prerogatives and powers. Either an irresponsible Congress, a body without a head, arrogates power to itself, and the President uses his veto power sparingly, takes no initiative in legislation and fails to utilize his powers of persuading public opinion (chiefly because public opinion regards all this as an "interference" with the proper sphere of Congress), or the situation is reversed, the President assumes dictatorial powers, and Congress becomes for the most part a mere rubber stamp. The first situation is essentially that which existed from the administration of Andrew Johnson to that of McKinley (though the two terms of Cleveland were partial exceptions). The second situation is that which has existed in recent years, and exists above all in wartime.

Thus, without essential change in the Constitution the pendulum has swung from congressional domination to presidential domination. This is not because the Constitution *itself* is "flexible," but precisely because it is inflexible. The nice "balance of powers" that it contemplates is unworkable. If the powers for obstruction that it grants are really exercised on all sides, the only possible result is paralysis. Our Constitution can be made to work only by the inability or the tacit refusal of either the executive or the legislature to exercise its nominal powers. This leads to an extreme, and one extreme is so unsatisfactory that it creates a demand for the other. Congressional dictatorship, because it is anonymous and headless, becomes intolerable; but presidential dictatorship, because it can act on the uncontrollable personal whim of one man, is far worse. A Congress must have a head; it must have recognized and responsible leaders. And the executive must have to consult his colleagues, and to submit his decisions to the representatives of the people, before he can act on them.

The most obvious democratic way to fuse the legislative and executive powers is to permit the legislative body itself to select the man who is to be at once its own leader and the executive. The legislature must have the power of electing him and the power of removing him at will. Only by this means can we be sure that the executive is always the real choice of the legislature, and that the legislature is therefore ready to accept and follow his leadership. Control, of course, must not exist only from the legislative side (as it did in the Third French Republic), because this weakens the executive, makes his tenure unstable, and allows the legislature to indulge in irresponsible caprice. Once selected, therefore, the executive (as in England) should have the reciprocal power, if the legislature votes a lack of confidence in him, to dissolve the legislature and force it to go with him to the voters of the country for an immediate decision between them. Faced by such a possibility, a legislature will think very carefully before voting lack of confidence in the executive so chosen. A situation like that in France, which had a new Premier on the average every few months, will become impossible; the Premier is more likely, as in England, to remain in office on the average for a number of years.

What are the constitutional barriers to such a government in the United States, and what are the minimum constitutional changes necessary to secure it? The leading obstacles to this reform may be set down as follows: (1) the constitutional separation of the legislature into two Houses *of approximately equal powers;* (2) the constitutionally fixed terms of office for the House of Representatives (and for the Senate, together with the fact that there is no way of forcing the whole Senate to stand for election at once, at the same time as the whole membership of the House); and (3) the veto and several other powers of the President.

Unless at least these three provisions are changed, responsible cabinet government is impossible. It is not difficult to see why. Let us consider them in order.

1. Responsible cabinet government is impossible as long as there are two legislative Houses, each of which can defeat the will of the other. The late Wil-

liam MacDonald, urging a parliamentary government for America, seemed to think that the main change needed to effect it was to elect the House and Senate at the same time.[1] This mistakes the real difficulty. As long as the two Houses of Congress have equal powers, any cabinet formed must have the constant support of *both* Houses. This would be peculiarly difficult to secure. MacDonald seemed to assume that if the two were elected at the same time, both would be virtually sure to have majorities of the same political party. But their radically different method of representation, as well as long experience with state legislatures, indicates that this by no means would follow. The lower and upper houses of state legislatures often differ in political complexion, even though elected at the same time—chiefly because their constituencies, and sometimes the basis of representation, are differently arranged. This difference is particularly likely to occur whenever the parties are nearly equal in popular strength. What should we do —even given full elections of each House at the same time—if we found a slight Republican majority in the House, for example, and a slight Democratic majority in the Senate? We might be forced immediately to call a second election. But repeated elections, though they would be expensive, vexatious, and disruptive to the nation's life, would give no assurance of solving the problem. The real need is to reduce the powers of the Senate. It should have the power only to force the House to reconsider a question—by obliging it,

[1] *A New Constitution for a New America* (1921), p. 63.

for example, to repass a measure by something more than a mere majority. But it should not be permitted to exercise, as now, an absolute veto. The cabinet should be chosen by the House alone. The problem otherwise created by a deadlock between the House and Senate, in the choice either of leaders or policies, would then not have to be considered.

2. The normal term of members of the House (I shall consider this question at more length later) might be profitably extended to four years, *but there should be no constitutional assurance of such a term.* Unless the House's chosen leader has the constitutional power to dissolve it at any time, we have seen that it is not possible to secure genuinely reponsible and stable cabinet government.

3. Parliamentary government contemplates that the legislature itself, under leadership of its own selection, shall formulate policy, and that its selected leadership shall be responsible for executing it. As a corollary of these requirements, a constitutional revision would have to remove from the President the veto power, the direct power to execute the laws, the power to make treaties, and the direction of military and naval policy. It is obvious that the veto power in its present form would have to be eliminated altogether. The other powers mentioned would be transferred to the chosen leader of Congress, whom I shall hereafter refer to as the "premier." [1]

---

[1] In proposing a parliamentary government, nomenclature presents a real problem for America, and I am unable to see any fully satisfactory solution of it. Traditionally, the office of President is the one with which we associate the greatest prestige and power. If we

These, it seems to me, are the minimum constitutional changes necessary to make genuine cabinet government possible.

are to reduce that office to the merely nominal headship of the State, as illustrated by the presidency of the French Third Republic, many Americans might resent it, or might fail to understand the nature of the new presidency because of their historic associations. The title of "premier," again, will not only seem strange because of its foreign derivation, but will suggest to many a prime *minister* essentially subordinate to a king or president. How are we to avoid these difficulties, however? To call our premier the "congressional leader" would describe him in well-understood and orthodox American terms; but this would be a clumsy title. We could hardly shorten it to "the leader," because that term has now gathered evil associations from its perversion in Germany and Italy to describe a despot. To call the congressional leader the "president" would involve serious confusions, particularly if we are to retain a permanent head of the State. What would the latter be called? To call either the congressional leader or the permanent head of the national State the "governor" would involve confusion with our present State heads bearing that title. "Premier" and "president" seem to remain, respectively, the best compromises. After all, in England, the King, which once meant the all but absolute ruler, has been—though in that case gradually—reduced to a ceremonial figurehead without any change of title to indicate the change of status.

VI

A RESPONSIBLE GOVERNMENT IN OUTLINE: I

IF WE wish to secure a government calculated to give the most satisfactory results, it will be desirable to adopt more than merely the minimum constitutional changes necessary to make cabinet government possible. The changes suggested in the last chapter could bring us abreast, let us say, of current British practice in government, with the advantage of having no hereditary monarchy or House of Lords. But if it willed to do so, America could once again, as in 1787, lead the world forward to new advances in political institutions. Let us, therefore, in the following three chapters examine from the beginning what improvements in governmental techniques we might make if we had the enterprise and courage to do so.

It is highly desirable, I think, that we should retain a written constitution, and that we should not, as the English do, rely upon a constitution that consists merely of an ill-defined group of basic documents, traditions, customs and vague understandings. An unwritten constitution, it is true, has the great advantage of flexibility: it permits prompt action in a crisis, and it does not embarrassingly restrict a government in choosing the best means of dealing with a problem. Against this, however, it has serious dangers. In a federation of states, as in our own country, Canada and Australia, a written constitution is needed to delimit clearly the respective spheres of action of the federal and state governments. But it is also an important safeguard (though it would be folly to consider it an absolute one) against headstrong action, usurpation of powers or tyranny. No legislature or executive should be allowed to consider itself omnipotent, or to be its own judge of the extent of its powers. It ought not to be able to prolong its own tenure of office purely by its own will. It ought not to be able to override or abridge those freedoms guaranteed by our Bill of Rights. The best institutional protection against all such usurpations is a written constitution interpreted by a judiciary independent of the executive and the legislature. But such a written constitution, if it is not in itself to be an evil, if it is not to breed schemes for evading or circumventing it, should not have the "unique inaccessibility to amendment" that Mr. Laski describes as characteristic of our own Constitution.[1] I have reserved to a special chapter a full discussion of the way in which the amending process could be made simple and prompt, instead of, as at present, cumbersome, dilatory and uncertain.

There may be some question whether, in discussing political institutions, it is more logical to begin with the executive or with the legislature; but because,

[1] *A Grammar of Politics* (1925), p. 305.

A RESPONSIBLE GOVERNMENT IN OUTLINE: I

as we have seen, the most satisfactory way to select the executive is *through* the legislature, it is more convenient to begin with a discussion of the latter.

The first question is how the legislature itself is to be selected. It ought to be selected, I think, by secret ballot and by "universal suffrage," with, however, certain qualifications. There should be no discrimination because of sex, race, color or "previous condition of servitude"; but obviously there must be discrimination because of age. Only persons who have reached maturity can be assumed to have the minimum of judgment necessary properly to exercise the right to vote. The American States are similarly justified in excluding from the franchise felons, idiots and lunatics. It is also altogether proper that the States should provide, as they do, that voters must be at least able to read and write. It would be desirable even to add the requirement that they should be able to perform elementary arithmetical operations. Educational qualifications might be raised still higher than this if it were not for the difficulty of assuring that the tests applied would be completely objective, and would really measure the sort of knowledge necessary for political judgment.

What is to be said of property qualifications, which existed for centuries in England and still exist in some local elections here? The argument in favor of property qualifications is plausible and at least deserves to be carefully weighed. Those with property, it is urged, are a great conservative force: they have a higher stake in good government and in stable government than those without property. Those without property, moreover, inevitably seek to use the government to give benefits to themselves at the expense of those who have the property; and there is no logical stopping place to this process short of a final general equality of wealth (or poverty). One illustration cited is that of the income tax. Until the remorseless demands of the defense program and the war forced a lowering of the exemptions, the income tax, which was the main source of the Federal revenues, applied only to one voter in every twenty-five. It was hence not surprising that Congress could with impunity squander funds, levy heavier and heavier taxes, and use the proceeds to distribute favors among the "have-nots." Those from whom the money was visibly taken were a negligible part of the voting population; those to whom it was visibly given a much larger part. It has been argued, in fact, not by supporters of the private-enterprise system but by Marxists, that universal suffrage and pure political democracy lead inevitably to socialism.[1]

These theoretical arguments are often accompanied by arguments from actual experience. It is no accident, it is urged, that our own democracy attracted its greatest figures to leadership in the early days of the Republic, or that British political life reached its highest level in the period of Gladstone and Disraeli or earlier, when men of the type of Burke, Macaulay, Cobden, Bright and Mill filled the halls of Parlia-

[1] See HAROLD J. LASKI, *Democracy in Crisis* (1933) and *Parliamentary Government in England* (1938).

ment; for it was precisely in these periods that the suffrage was restricted by property and other qualifications, and first-rate statesmen, rather than demagogic politicians, were elected. And in present-day America, it has been contended, it is noteworthy that a State like Virginia, which has a poll tax, accounts for a very high proportion of the few able men in Congress, compared with the total number of men it sends there.

Plausible as some of these arguments are, I do not think they make a convincing case for restriction of the voting privilege on property grounds. When the franchise is restricted to any group of citizens, it tends to be used mainly in the interests of that group. The men and women of property cannot be counted upon to cast their votes also in the interests of persons without property, or to recognize fully what the legitimate interests and grievances of the latter group are. The exclusion of any group from a voice in the government is likely only to turn that group into permanent malcontents. The main cure of the situation complained of is not a restriction of the voting privilege, but improvement in the political and economic education of those to whom the voting privilege is extended. And the ballot is itself both an incentive and a means to improve this education.

Nevertheless, there are certain important qualifications that must be considered. John Stuart Mill, writing in 1860, contended that "the assembly which votes the taxes, either general or local, should be elected exclusively by those who pay something towards the taxes imposed. Those who pay no taxes, disposing by their votes of other people's money, have every motive to be lavish and none to economize. As far as money matters are concerned, any power of voting possessed by them is a violation of the fundamental principle of free government; a severance of the power of control from the interest in its beneficial exercise. It amounts to allowing them to put their hands into other people's pockets for any purpose which they think fit to call a public one; which in some of the great towns of the United States is known to have produced a scale of local taxation onerous beyond example, and wholly borne by the wealthier classes." This passage, written eighty years ago, seems prophetic of present conditions. "Representation," Mill held, "should be co-extensive with taxation, not stopping short of it, but also not going beyond it." But the way to bring about this situation, as he saw, was not to restrict the suffrage but to extend the field of taxation: "It is essential, as it is on many other accounts desirable, that taxation, in a visible shape, should descend to the poorest class." Indirect taxes on consumption, he saw, such as those on tea, coffee, sugar, tobacco and liquor, are not properly felt for this purpose. He suggested that "a small direct annual payment, rising and falling with the gross expenditure of the country, should be required from every registered elector; that so every one might feel that the money which he assisted in voting was partly his own, and that he was interested in keeping down its amount." [1]

2

There is one restriction of the suffrage, however, that it seems to me both highly just and highly important to make. This is to remove the voting privilege from governmental officeholders for as long as they continue to hold office. The reason for this is that officeholders, through their very function, already exercise a far more than proportionate influence on governmental policy compared with other citizens. Officeholders as a class, moreover, almost invariably vote as a unit, and they vote in the main for one thing —to keep themselves in office and to increase the benefits of office. This bloc vote is a tremendously important factor in swinging an otherwise close election.

And the typical American election is close. This fact is commonly concealed by our lazy and vicious national habit of always counting, predicting and publicizing election results in terms of the numerical "plurality" gained by the winning candidate over the candidate that ran second, and almost never in terms of the respective percentage of the total vote gained by each candidate. But in innumerable local and state elections, and in the crucial States in presidential elections, the typical swing from victory to defeat for Democrats and Republicans is a change, say, from 52 per cent for the Democrats and 48 per cent for Re-

[1] *Representative Government* (Everyman ed.), pp. 281-282.

publicans to 52 per cent for the Republicans and 48 per cent for the Democrats.[1]

In such a situation the officeholders will commonly retain the power to keep themselves in office by their own votes. And experience as well as common sense shows that that is the purpose for which they use their votes. This block of officeholders forms the nucleus, the very backbone of the great city machines, the state machines, and an ominously growing Federal machine. It nearly always controls the primaries. It nearly always controls any election in which the public interest is small. It determines every otherwise close election. It is not difficult for the machine to "get out the vote" of the officeholders, because their very means of livelihood depends directly upon whether and how they vote. To the average citizen the issues in a particular election may seem abstract and unintelligible, but they are never so to the officeholders.

This body of officeholders not only votes invariably to keep itself in office; it votes as a unit to increase its pay or to prevent reductions in pay; and it makes its decisions, not in the general interest, but in its own. In practically every city in America the po-

[1] An elementary statistical study, from this standpoint, of past election results, and a change in newspaper habits of reporting results, so that they could be immediately seen in percentage terms as well as plurality terms, would do a great deal to clarify this question in the public mind. Many supposed "landslides" would shrink considerably in dimensions under such analysis. In the Coolidge "landslide," Coolidge received only 54 per cent of the total vote. In the Roosevelt "landslide" over Willkie, Mr. Roosevelt received only 55 per cent of the total vote.

licemen, the firemen, the street cleaners, the teachers have powerful organizations. They are constantly demanding more pay, shorter hours, longer vacations, bigger pensions, or fighting any effort to reduce whatever advantages they may have secured. They threaten the defeat of any politician who fails to support their demands. They control a solid block of votes, and almost no politician dares to stand up to them, unless his city is actually known to be facing bankruptcy, or unless the demands have become so obviously extravagant as to arouse an active and unmistakable public resentment. The result is that these groups succeed in securing for themselves fantastic vacation and pension privileges which the generality of citizens do not remotely enjoy.

This evil, serious enough throughout our history, has been a growing one, and now grows at an accelerative pace. As government takes over more and more functions, controls the individual's life more and more, it adds correspondingly to its personnel. It is sometimes difficult to say whether this growth in the bureaucracy is an incidental result of growth of governmental powers, or whether it is the other way round. Certainly many schemes to increase governmental control originate in the basic desire to create more political jobs, to increase the already tremendous power of patronage. The higher the percentage of the total vote in the hands of the body of office-holders, the greater is their power to keep themselves in office, and the smaller is the power of the rest of the citizenry to control affairs or to change those who control affairs.

The clear solution of this problem is to disfranchise the governmental officeholders as long as they continue to hold office. There is here not the slightest possibility of injustice, for the officeholders would continue nonetheless to exercise a far greater influence on and control of public policy than any other group. The disfranchisement, moreover, would be a limited one not only in time but in scope. Officeholders should be denied the right to vote only in elections within the field of their own jurisdiction. City and state officeholders, for example, should retain the right to vote for Federal officeholders; Federal officeholders, the right to vote in city and state elections, and so on.

This limited disfranchisement, it is true, would not cure the evil against which it is directed; it would merely mitigate it. For the officeholders' wives, parents, grown children, brothers, sisters, cousins and aunts would also, in the main, probably vote in what the office holders conceived to be their direct interest. It would obviously be both administratively difficult and unfair in policy to attempt to disfranchise whole families. All this is no argument, however, for not taking a step that would be in itself reasonable, and would at least reduce the dimensions of the evil.

To those not convinced of the need for this step, I suggest a temporary compromise. Let officeholders vote as heretofore; let them vote individually by secret ballot as heretofore; but segregate their vote in special ballot boxes or machines from that of the other voters. I feel confident that, once the great body of voters were able to see in this way the solidity of the officeholder vote and the way in which it affects elections, they would support the kind of limited disfranchisement here suggested.

But if this principle is sound for officeholders, it may be asked, should it not be extended? If it is desirable to remove the voting privilege from officeholders on the ground that they already have the greatest influence on governmental policy and a direct and unified interest in keeping themselves in power, what about farmers living on direct government subsidies? What about people on relief? What about corporations with government contracts or tariff protection? I agree that the same principle applies to these cases, but the administrative difficulties of applying the proposal are here very great—above all the practical difficulty of knowing exactly where and how to draw the line. John Stuart Mill regarded it

... as required by first principles, that the receipt of parish relief should be a peremptory disqualification for the franchise. He who cannot by his labor suffice for his own support has no claim to the privilege of helping himself to the money of others. By becoming dependent on the remaining members of the community for actual subsistence, he abdicates his claim to equal rights with them in other respects. Those to whom he is indebted for the continuance of his very existence may justly claim the exclusive management of those common concerns, to which he now brings nothing, or less than he takes away.[1]

Such considerations might be dismissed today as of merely academic importance, were it not for the sheer numbers in receipt of direct subsidies or direct relief. They constitute a formidable army of votes, an army capable of controlling elections; and their votes are cast for the continuance of their subsidies and relief receipts, and for an enlargement of the amount. Their welfare depends upon these in so direct and immediate a manner that they cannot mistake it. The rest of the voters, however, who partially or wholly support them, cannot have the same direct perception of what these subsidy and relief payments are costing them. The incidence of all except direct personal income taxes is obscure or disputable, and relief payments are not segregated in the tax bill. Hence, humanitarian considerations apart, there is never the same tightly organized and unitary opinion against relief increases as in favor of them. That is why professional politicians cannot stand up against agitation for relief increases.

But if we are to restrict the franchise in this direction, where are we to begin and end? How much relief should disqualify for the franchise, and over what period? Mill held that "as a condition of the franchise, a term should be fixed, say five years previous to the registry, during which the applicant's name has

[1] *Ibid.*, p. 282.

not been on the parish books as a recipient of relief." No one would take so stern a view today; nor is there any need to. I suggest as possibly a workable formula something like this: All recipients of direct government subsidies or relief, if received within ninety days of an election, and if in the preceding year the sums received had exceeded one-half of the recipient's total income, would be disqualified from voting in that particular election. Also, the officers and directors of any corporation, more than one-half of whose orders consisted of government contracts in a similar period, would also be disqualified from voting in that particular election.

Such a formula, I confess, would draw an arbitrary line. But arbitrary lines are constantly and necessarily drawn by law and governmental regulation—the voting age of twenty-one, the qualifications for old-age pensions, the qualifications, indeed, for relief and subsidy payments themselves. I am ready to admit, also, that such a formula would only mitigate and not remove the evil with which it attempts to deal—the evil of solid bodies of voters on the government pay roll, voting to keep themselves there. But it is better merely to reduce an evil than not to do anything about it at all.

3

Having decided who should be qualified or disqualified to vote for members of the legislature, the next logical question is how should such qualified electors vote? I have already explained in Chap. III (in discussing the reasons why the German and Italian governmental systems broke down), why the legislature should not be elected by a system of proportional representation. It encourages a multiplicity of parties; it encourages extremists; it "splinters the electorate" (to use a phrase of Harry D. Gideonse'); it tends to be an instrument of disintegration. The majority system, on the other hand, encourages the spirit of compromise essential to democracy, and permits action, a coherent policy and a stable government. But the ordinary plurality system of voting can be improved upon to bring it much nearer to a true majority system. In a later chapter I shall suggest a method of voting designed to do this.

There is not much that can be usefully said about the qualifications of members of the legislature except that there should be no arbitrary restrictions on the voters' range of choice. The residential qualification in our Constitution has been particularly harmful in this respect. It is discussed at length in a later chapter. The various age qualifications in our Federal and state constitutions probably do little harm and certainly little good. Let us remember that William Pitt the younger entered Parliament at twenty-one and was Chancellor of the Exchequer at twenty-three, and did rather well. There seems no good reason why the age limit for any official need be placed above twenty-five. A high educational qualification, again, would discriminate in favor of the wealthy and against many able men of great political judgment.

There are two provisions, however, that would be likely to raise the quality of the legislature. One would be a restriction of its numbers. The other would be the fullest opportunities for able men to exercise influence and to secure promotion to posts of greater responsibility. Obviously the first provision is an important step in securing the second.

Nearly all modern legislatures are too large. They are too large to function efficiently, to command public respect, or to attract the most able men. The American House of Representatives consists of 435 members; the British House of Commons, of 615; the French Chamber of Deputies consisted of 618. My own conviction is that there is no good reason why the house of a national legislature should consist of more than about 150 members. Nothing is gained by enlargement beyond this point, and a great deal is lost. A hundred and fifty members, certainly, are enough to prevent dangerous concentration of power. It is often said that the districts from which members are elected should be small enough so that the member is known to the district and does not lose touch with it. This argument is unrealistic, and under modern conditions presupposes almost the contrary of the actual situation. Ask the average voter in any large city who his Congressman is, and the chances are more than nine out of ten that he will be unable to tell you. But he is far more likely to know the names of the two Senators from his State: they are more prominent men; he reads more about them and even knows something about what their policies are.

Representatives, by being numerous, become anonymous. They become simply part of a great mob.

They have next to no opportunity to take part in the debates—unless they happen to be among the very few who head committees—and so the average voter never comes to know what their capacities are in that direction. Because they are part of a great mob, also, they have few opportunities to function usefully in other directions. The result of this (combined with the deplorable internal organization of Congress) is that few able men are any longer attracted to a career in the House. The more men there are in a legislative assembly, the less work one can find (after a few key positions have been filled) for each of them to do. And, as Bagehot has pointed out, if you employ even "the best set of men to do nearly nothing, they will quarrel with each other about that nothing." [1]

It is no mere accident that the American House of Representatives attracted a far higher type of man, on the average, when it was far smaller than at present. The original House consisted of only sixty-four members. In the period of 1827 to 1831, when such figures as Webster, Clay and Calhoun were in Congress, the House had still grown only to 213 members.

The larger the House, in brief, the less opportunity each individual member has either to occupy an important committee post or to participate in the debates. Either the debates have to be indefinitely prolonged, to provide this opportunity, or (and this is the actual consequence in most cases) the large House has to adopt stringent rules confining debate arbi-

[1] *The English Constitution*, p. 231.

trarily to a few chosen leaders, or restricting the individual speeches of other members far short of the length necessary to make important points effectively. As a result of this policy on the part of the House of Representatives—a policy made necessary purely by its great numbers—the average Representative is a nobody. On the other hand, the prolonged opportunity for debate of the average Senator—a policy made possible only by the comparatively small numbers (ninety-six) in the upper House—make that average Senator a Somebody. Able and ambitious men seldom seek election to an assembly in which they become nobodies, and in which, moreover, their chance to become a Somebody is indefinitely postponed because of the vicious seniority system in Congress.

4

This brings us to the highly important question of the internal organization of the legislative body. This internal organization may be partly a matter of written constitutional provisions, and partly a matter of custom and informal agreement. I shall discuss what I think the most satisfactory practices are likely to be, only in a few cases raising the question of whether or not it is desirable to make any particular practice obligatory through a constitutional provision or to leave it to be established by agreement. In certain cases it will be obvious that a given practice or form of organization should be prescribed by the Constitution. In other cases it will be equally obvious that custom and informal agreement are all that are either necessary or desirable to support a practice. There will be, however, some border-line cases.

The first task of the legislative assembly when it meets will be to choose a premier. How shall he be chosen? The usual procedure in cabinet government, when a new parliament has been elected, is for the king or the constitutional president, the nominal head of the state, to "consult" with the "leaders" of the parliament, and either to "take their advice" about who should be premier, or to "use his own discretion" in choosing a premier and asking him to "form a government."

What are the advantages and disadvantages of this procedure as compared with its possible alternatives? It is not difficult to imagine, for example, an arrangement under which the "president" would have no discretion in choosing a premer, that function being cared for by direct election by the members of the legislative assembly itself. It is also possible to imagine a parliamentary government in which the traditional office occupied by the king or president did not even exist—in which, for example, the parliamentary leader himself took over the title of president. What is to be said, comparatively, about these two different arrangements, or possibly for some compromise between them?

The traditional arrangement, let us recall, is the result less of deliberate contrivance than of historic accident. The English King was originally the real and not merely the nominal source of power: the ministers were indeed merely his ministers; he was their real and not merely their nominal appointor; they really did merely "advise" him, and not, as they do today, in fact instruct him. Certainly if we were starting afresh, the direct selection of the premier by the parliament would seem the simplest, most direct and most natural arrangement. The leader so chosen would be certain to be the real and the first choice of the parliament. Again and again a king or a president possessing discretion has misused that discretion. For that reason the British, though retaining the fiction of royal discretion, have in fact reduced it to the narrowest limits. King Victor Emmanuel used his discretion very doubtfully in allowing Mussolini to come into power, and the aged President Hindenburg used his disastrously in appointing Hitler. The minimum lesson of these developments is that the discretion of the permanent head of the state in such matters should be reduced to the narrowest practicable limits.

If a parliament consists of only two great parties, the method of selecting the leader presents no problems. Each party will no doubt already have its chosen leader; if it has not, it can easily choose one in caucus. Whether there is a choice by election within the parliament or by a president with limited discretion, the result will be the same: the premier will be the leader of the majority party.

Where there is a multiplicity of parties, however, the decision will be more difficult. I suggest that the following procedure might most usefully be followed: The various parties or groups should nominate their candidates. They should then vote for the premier by secret ballot. This vote should be conducted either by the majority acceptance system to be explained in Chap. IX or by some other majority preferential system. The result of the balloting should then be announced to the parliament. If, in the opinion of any considerable group, the result is not decisive enough to indicate a clear choice, this may be followed by a second ballot. With this second ballot before him, the president should select a premier and ask him to form a cabinet.

This procedure, I believe, would have several advantages. It would determine the real sentiment of the members of the house concerning their choice for premier. A secret ballot seems desirable to reduce personal feuds as much as possible within the parliament, and to reduce efforts of the chosen leaders to reward those who had voted for them and punish those who had voted against them. The secret ballot, in short, would perform the same function for a parliament in this particular choice as it does for the electorate at large: it would allow a man to cast an unintimidated vote in accordance with his real convictions. The primary choice of the premier, in this case, would rest with the parliament, as it should. But where that choice was not altogether clear, the president would have some discretion, among the contenders, in naming a possible premier most likely to be acceptable.

In choosing a premier, the legislative body would be almost certain to choose one of its own members;

but it should not be constitutionally limited to this choice. In theory, it should be able to go outside itself, just as our party presidential nominating conventions now do, and choose anyone in the country. This follows from the principle appealed to in condemning the residential qualifications for Congress members: there should be no arbitrary restrictions on the range of choice. It is at least possible that in a certain crisis someone not a member of the legislature may be regarded by the legislature itself as its best leader. (He might be, for example, a former leader retired from active politics.) In such a case the legislature should not be stopped either by constitutional or rigid traditional barriers from naming him. A premier so chosen should have the same rights and powers (including the right to a vote) as a premier originally chosen from within the legislative body.

When the premier has been named, his first duty will be to select a cabinet. Because of the sort of work it has to do, this body should be compact. It ought not to exceed ten or twelve men, a number described by Sir Robert Peel as ideal for a cabinet, because this number of men could sit around a table and all take an effective part in deliberation. His own cabinet of 1841-1846 had thirteen members. A cabinet of twenty-eight to thirty-two, as at present in Great Britain, begins to approximate, as Ramsay Muir points out, a public meeting.[1] (The present "War Cabinet," however, within the larger Cabinet, consists of only nine men.)

[1] Cf. *How Britain Is Governed* (3d ed., 1935), p. 108.

The premier will probably, in fact, choose mainly members of the legislature itself; but like the legislature in choosing the premier, the premier in choosing the cabinet should be free to go outside the legislature for members. Such a privilege would be of more practical importance than any theoretical right of the legislature to go outside itself in choosing a premier, because it is a privilege that is more likely in fact to be used. The cabinet often calls for men of highly specialized ability, and for a particular task no such man may be found in the legislature. The best man may be outside. The premier in such a case should have the power of making use of his talents. Members of the cabinet chosen from outside the legislature should, once accepted by the legislature, have the same right to vote as if they had been elected.

This voting power, if used in moderation, would accomplish much good and little harm. It is often desirable, for the sake of stable government, that a majority be slightly over-represented. To prevent abuse of this privilege, the legislative majority or the premier should be constitutionally limited regarding the number of votes he could thus add. With a total cabinet limited, however, to, say, 10 men in addition to the premier, there could be no serious "packing" of a legislative body of 150 or more members, even if the total cabinet consisted of men chosen from outside the legislature. And as a practical possibility, no legislative majority would be likely to tolerate a cabinet that was not drawn in the main from its own members; for at least several leaders of the majority would expect to be chosen for the cabinet.

When the premier—or, as we might more accurately call him up to this point, the man asked to form a government—had chosen his cabinet, he would present it to the legislature, which would then vote whether to accept or reject it as a body. This vote should obviously be a public one by the members of the legislature. They may properly vote by secret ballot when policy is in a formative stage, and in many cases it is actually desirable that they should so vote; but the public has a right to know where each of its representatives in the legislature stands on any major decision when it is finally adopted.

It is not difficult to see why the cabinet should be selected in the manner just indicated. Bagehot called the cabinet "a committee of the legislature"; but clearly by far the most important member of that committee is the premier. He is the real executive head of the government. Therefore he should be chosen by the legislature first, without confusing the question by choosing other individuals with him. He is the keystone of the whole arch. Once he has been chosen, it is obviously he who should have the main decision in choosing his colleagues. He must be able to choose those who he feels will work best with him. What is most important about his cabinet is not that it shall contain the highest percentage of men of individual brilliance, but that it shall work best as a team. It must be a harmonious team consisting of men ready to follow the premier's leadership and to accept the roles assigned to them. The premier will necessarily have to consult the sentiments of his party in the legislature and conciliate if he cannot satisfy the more influential members of that party; but the initiative in choice for membership in the cabinet should remain with him.

VII

A RESPONSIBLE GOVERNMENT IN OUTLINE: II

IF IT is assumed that a cabinet, *i.e.*, a "government," has been formed and accepted, what ought to be its functions? The members of the cabinet, clearly, though each will probably be responsible for some particular department of government, ought not to be immersed in routine or detail. The premier certainly ought not to occupy any other position in the cabinet. His function is to lead and to coordinate the other members of the cabinet. He must bear the chief responsibility for the major policies adopted—though obviously he should not adopt these policies until after consultation with his cabinet colleagues, and usually not until even wider consultation. The other members of the cabinet should keep constantly in mind the dictum of Sir George Lewis, who at different times served as British Chancellor of the Exchequer, Home Secretary, and Minister for War: "It is not the business of a cabinet minister to work his department. His business is to see that it is properly worked." [1]

[1] Quoted by WALTER BAGEHOT, *The English Constitution*, p. 177.

To help the cabinet member follow this policy, a change in customary governmental titles seems desirable. Both in England and here the official who serves immediately under the Cabinet Secretary is called the Under Secretary. It has been the practice of the British to appoint a permanent, skilled under-secretariat; and we have made some partial efforts in that direction. The chief function of the Under Secretary has been or should be to carry on the actual routine administration of his department; the chief function of the cabinet member has been or should be to formulate the major policies of the department. (Sometimes the cabinet member must know something of details in order intelligently to formulate broad policies; on the other hand, the Under Secretary's great knowledge of details will be useful in helping him to advise on broad policies. But all this does not change the essential division of labor involved.) It would probably help both the under-secretariat and the cabinet members to bear in mind their respective functions better, as well as help the public to understand the real division of function and responsibility, if the permanent head of each department, who did the actual administrative work, had the title of "Administrator" of the department instead of "Under Secretary." The cabinet member, the Secretary, would then feel more free to devote himself to settling broad questions of policy and could prevent himself from getting buried in routine.

In addition to seeing that the administrative and executive work of the government is being properly carried out, the chief function of the cabinet will be to formulate the major bills to be submitted to the full legislature. The members of the cabinet will discuss with each other, with experts in the government departments, and often with non-governmental experts, the broad policy that ought to be adopted regarding a problem. They will then delegate experts in special fields in the departments, as well as general drafting experts, to prepare a bill. When the bill has been prepared, the cabinet will meet with the chief experts who have framed it, consider its main provisions, decide whether it needs amendments to be drafted on the spot or referred back to the experts for drafting, and then decide whether or not to adopt the completed bill as the cabinet's policy.

If it is assumed that such a cabinet bill has been adopted, what should be the next step? I suggest it would be desirable, before such a bill reached the full legislature, that it pass through two more stages. The first would be its submission to a legislative council chosen to represent the whole legislative body. The cabinet, by its method of selection, will almost necessarily represent only the majority in the legislature. On the legislative council the minority should also be represented, in proportion to its numbers in the legislature.

There are several ways in which this council might be chosen. It might consist, say, of only a dozen men, chosen by the legislature by secret ballot and proportional representation. (The objections to P.R. as a method of choosing the legislature itself would not apply to this special use of the device; for a plurality or majority method of voting would already have prevented the splintering of the electorate and legislature that is the vice of P.R.) It is important for the special function that the council is to perform that it should be essentially a *miniature* of the legislature, and that the legislature should accept it as such. For leadership and initiative in action, moreover, the cabinet, which is the *majority* in miniature, would already exist under this arrangement, and would ordinarily be much more powerful than the council.

The council might, however, be chosen by less formal methods. The minority party or parties might be permitted to choose their representatives on the council in proportion to their membership in the legislature, while the cabinet itself could represent the legislative majority on the council. Suppose, for example, that the cabinet consisted of a dozen members, and that it represented a party with a majority of three-fifths in the legislature. Then in the council the full cabinet would represent the majority, while the minority party (or parties) would be entitled to choose two-fifths, or eight members more, for the council. These eight members would then represent, so to speak, the "cabinet" of the minority. They would presumably consist of the minority's ablest members. They would have the right to consult or to cross-examine the government experts in the departments who had helped to frame a cabinet bill. Funds would be made available to them so that they could choose their own special or permanent experts, and would not have to depend on the particular experts chosen by the cabinet or the "government."

2

A bill adopted by the cabinet would be submitted next to the council. It is highly desirable that the council, like the usual cabinet and like the present standing committees in Congress, should discuss bills in executive session—*i.e.*, in private and not in public. If demagogy, exhibitionist oratory and professional party strife are to be kept to a minimum, there would be nothing to be gained and much to be lost by public sessions of the council. The purpose at this stage would be to acquaint the minority's representatives with the bills to be proposed by the cabinet, to discuss the intent of these bills with them, and to allow them to make suggestions for amendment.

Such a process would benefit the majority, the minority, and the nation. There are liable to be in all bills, even the best meant, unintended jokers and other provisions that would work badly. If these are pointed out by the minority after the cabinet has already publicly committed itself to a bill, the majority may defend and retain them in order to save face, though it would quickly and willingly enough have removed some of them if it did not already feel publicly committed or if it did not appear to be *forced* to change them. The minority, therefore, may exercise more real influence in executive session than in public session.

But, it may be declared, this is not what the minority wants. It does not want real influence in legislation unless it gets public credit for it. It would rather that the cabinet submitted a bad bill, full of jokers, inconsistencies and loopholes, so that it could have the pleasure and advantage of deriding or denouncing these in the public session of the full legislature. What the minority wants is not influence out of power: it wants to get into power; and the more incompetent, ridiculous or dangerous it can make the majority appear, the more satisfied it will be. The minority will therefore withhold attempts to change bad provisions or kill bad bills in executive session of the council, in order that it may have the advantage of exposing these in public in the legislature.

This view is unduly cynical, and overlooks important factors in the situation. It assumes an almost complete lack of unselfish public spirit on the part of the minority. Moreover, it is by no means clear that it would be to the advantage of the minority to withhold private criticism. The cabinet would be in a position to say that the minority representatives had had an opportunity to point out defects in the bill in executive session of the council and had failed to do so. Moreover, it is not to the advantage of the minority that the cabinet-sponsored bills presented to the legislature should have too many defects. If the minority can remove incidental, unintended or unimportant defects from a bill that is fundamentally bad in principle, it will be free, in the public debate in the legislature, to concentrate on this fundamental unsoundness, without confusing the issue or the public mind with other considerations.

Nor does it help the minority to have too many objections to a bill, even if they are all justified. For a public that has not studied the matter closely will simply get the impression that the minority "objects to everything," "opposes everything," can "see no good in anything," "hates" the administration, and consists of nothing but professional faultfinders and carping scolds. Paradoxical as it may seem, it actually gives a political advantage to a government to exceed a certain point of badness, because it places the minority in this dilemma. The minority, to keep a repute for fairness, is almost obliged to concede "*some* good things" that the government in power has done.

This the device of the council will enable the minority to do. It can eliminate in private discussion unintended defects. It can endorse some bills wholly, making them non-partisan and "non-controversial," and so speed their progress through the full legislature. The minority will then be able to concentrate its opposition on a few crucial bills, and on the basic principle rather than the merely incidental defects of those bills. This will clarify questions in the public mind. The educational function of a legislature will hence be much better performed. When an election comes, the public is more likely to know what "the real issue" is; for if the minority raises too many issues, it will only confuse the public and will be accused of "floundering for an issue."

When a bill has passed the council, a written report should be prepared upon it. This should give a condensed summary and explanation of the bill's contents, together with a statement of the purpose of and need for the bill. In "non-controversial" bills this report may be unanimous. But where the cabinet and the minority are divided, as they often will be, the cabinet should summarize the argument for, and the minority the argument against, the bill. Each member of the legislature should receive a copy of the bill and of this report, and both should be available for public distribution to interested persons. This is the technique already commonly followed by the chief committees of Congress in "reporting out" a bill. It is an excellent educational device. A summary of a bill and of the arguments for and against it is not only an immense time saver for the individual legislative member, but for newspaper editors and others who help to shape and inform public opinion, and who wish to inform themselves at first hand. This summary is more likely to perform an educational service, indeed, than the actual debates in the full legislature, which are enormously verbose, while three-quarters of what is said there is likely to be either repetitious or uninformed.

When the council has passed a bill and submitted its report, the bill should be ready, after one further stage, for submission to the full legislature. The members of the cabinet will be occupied the year round, and this may be to a large extent true also of the minority members of the council. The minority should be represented by a body that the cabinet can always consult quickly in a crisis, or when some important decision is to be taken, in order that it may judge the probable opinion of the full legislature. (Because of their need to be constantly available, and of the extra burdens of work placed upon them, the minority members of the council, for as long as they serve in this position, should receive higher salaries than the ordinary members of the legislature, though lower salaries than members of the cabinet.) The full legislature, however, should not be expected to remain in constant session. At the very least, the members should have frequent opportunities to return to and consult their constituencies, for their very representative character depends upon their keeping in close touch with the needs and sentiments of their constituencies.

It is not desirable, moreover, that the legislature should consist wholly of "professional politicians." It should enlist, if possible, active lawyers, journalists, manufacturers, merchants, farmers, labor leaders, who will make their ability and experience available; and these should not be compelled wholly to abandon their former activities. One reason for the generally admitted qualitative superiority of the British Parliament to the American Congress is that the former contains a smaller percentage of purely professional politicians and a larger percentage of persons mainly engaged in other activities. This result is more easily achieved in England than here, however, not only because the seat of Government there is also the country's largest city and business center, but because the country is so much smaller, and members of Parliament can return to their constituencies more easily and more often.

3

When the full legislature meets, under the system here suggested, the council will already have passed nearly all the main bills to be considered. Not only will the legislature and the country know what most of the legislative program is to be; they will have before them official summaries of the arguments for and against it. Interests directly affected will know what is in store for them, and will be granted time to study the proposals and to prepare to support or oppose them. When the legislature meets, therefore, the various bills should be referred to special or standing committees of the legislature for further study.

These special or standing committees, as I conceive them, would be similar to those that already exist in Congress. There would, however, be some essential differences. Their individual powers would be substantially reduced. They would not normally be the centers for originating or framing measures to be presented to the legislature, but only the centers for revising measures. They would not present the results of their work directly to the legislature but merely *back* to the council and the cabinet. For if we are to have responsible government, if we are to know whom to hold accountable for what is either good or bad, responsibility must be centralized; and the place to centralize it is in the cabinet. This becomes impossible if, as in our Congress as at present constituted, legislation may originate in any one of eighty standing committees, each insulated from all the rest, each proposing legislation without regard to what other committees are proposing. As a result, all work at cross purposes with each other; no consistent pattern is traceable in legislation; and there is, in fact, no such thing as a legislative *program* at all, except insofar as this can be imposed by a strongly intrenched President. It is different, however, if these committees pass on bills that originate in the cabinet, and then merely try to get the results of their study accepted by the cabinet.

At present the first weeks of a Congressional session are usually thrown away while the great body of Congress sits around waiting for its committees to prepare legislation to submit to it. Under the form of organization here suggested, the cabinet, after legislation has passed through the council, will prepare a program or timetable, listing the order in which bills will be presented to the full legislature. It might use the early days of the legislative session to submit to the full legislature "non-controversial" bills, *i.e.*, cabinet bills adopted by unanimous vote of the council. It might be understood that these need not be submitted to any of the various legislative committees unless the chairman of one of these, as a result of a majority vote of his committee, asks the right to examine such a bill. In this way most of such bills might be got out of the way at the beginning of a session instead of being passed hastily and blindly at the end. Where, however, one measure is of particular urgency, the cabinet may give notice that it is to be presented at the very opening of the full legislative session. In such a case the members of the appropriate legislative committee, to consider that bill, would have to meet a few weeks before the full legislature.

The legislative committees, as now, would hold public hearings on the measures submitted to them by the cabinet or council. Since these committees would not, as at present, themselves have prepared this legislation, it is likely that they would give a more open-minded hearing to objections and constructive criticisms than they do now. After these hearings, the legislative committee would discuss the bill, decide whether it approved or disapproved of it, and what amendments, if any, it would submit to the council. All these would be decisions taken in executive session, not public decisions. The committee would then meet with the council, and its proposed amendments would be discussed, with the cabinet retaining full power of acceptance or rejection. When a final bill had been agreed upon, it would be submitted to the full legislature. It would then at last be open to public "full dress" debate.

Let us see what would have been accomplished by the procedure so far. The cabinet would have full responsibility for initiating legislation, and would be responsible for the legislation as finally submitted. But it would have had every opportunity to learn, both from the minority on the council, and from the legislative committees made up mainly of members of its own party, the faults of the legislation. It would have had every opportunity to correct these privately, when it could still do so with grace and without loss of prestige.

There would be other gains. Because responsibility must be centered, and because policy must be consistent, it is proper that normally all important bills should originate in the cabinet. But precisely because the cabinet must pass on *all* bills, its members will not have the opportunity for specialized study. This is exactly what the members of the special legislative committees, one on taxation, one on military affairs, one on agriculture, one on the judiciary, and so forth, will have. This organization will also give nearly every member of the legislature an opportunity to function at least in some special field. It is only by allowing members to utilize their talents that a legislature can attract talented members.

When the debate on a bill begins in the legislature, it is impossible, if the legislature is a large one, to give every member an opportunity to talk at length on the bill. But although the main discussion will come from the cabinet minister in charge of the bill, and although the opposition will probably be led by some selected member of the minority on the council, special opportunities for discussion should also be given to the members of the particular legislative committee that has considered a bill. In this way the debates are likely to be genuinely informative, for those who play the main part in participating in them will already have had ample opportunity to study the bill under discussion.

One final word needs to be said about the legislative committees here suggested. They will be selected for the most part as congressional committees are selected, with majorities and minorities in proportion to those in the whole legislature, but they will not adhere to the vicious principle of "seniority." On this principle, now followed in all the standing committees of Congress, the member of the majority party on that committee who has served longest in Congress becomes the chairman, regardless of his ability or his competence, and regardless of how his views on the subject may conform with those of the Administration. This principle has nothing to recommend it. It has been the source of great mischief. The chairman of such a committee should be selected either by the cabinet, or, perhaps preferably, by a secret ballot of the members of the committee itself. In this way he would be most likely to represent the committee's views, or the committee's own estimate regarding which was its ablest member.

4

We have arrived at the point at which the bill is before the full legislature. The council has allowed a certain tentative maximum period for debate. The principles of the bill will be discussed as a whole, special clauses will be questioned, amendments will be suggested. What policy is to be followed regarding the latter? The proper answer, I think, must rest on the distinction drawn by John Stuart Mill between "the function of making laws, for which a numerous popular assembly is radically unfit, and that of getting good laws made, which is its proper duty and cannot be satisfactorily fulfilled by any other authority." [1] Mill had stated this idea in expanded form in his *Representative Government:*

A numerous assembly is as little fitted for the direct business of legislation as for that of administration. There is hardly any kind of intellectual work which so much needs to be done, not only by experienced and exercised minds, but by minds trained to the task through long and laborious study, as the business of making laws. This is a sufficient reason, were there no other, why they can never be well made but by a committee of very few persons. A reason no less conclusive is, that every provision of a law requires to be framed with the most accurate and long-sighted perception of its effect on all the other provisions; and the law when made should be capable of fitting into a consistent whole with the previously existing laws. It is impossible that these conditions should be in any degree fulfilled when laws are voted clause by clause in a miscellaneous assembly. The incongruity of such a mode of legislating would strike all minds, were it not that our laws are already, as to form and construction, such a chaos, that the confusion and contradiction seem incapable of being made greater by any addition to the mass.[2]

Who is not familiar with the picture that Mill draws of what happens when a bill of many clauses is open to amendment by the whole legislative assem-

[1] *Autobiography* (1873), (World's Classics ed.), p. 224.
[2] Everyman ed., p. 235.

bly? "Clauses omitted which are essential to the working of the rest; incongruous ones inserted to conciliate some private interest, or some crotchety member who threatens to delay the bill; articles foisted in on the motion of some sciolist with a mere smattering of the subject," etc.? [1]

What is the cure for this? Mill suggested that laws should be framed by a single permanent legislative commission, and submitted to the full legislature to be accepted or rejected in their totality. But this is for several reasons impracticable and undesirable. All bills ought to be framed by drafting experts to assure that they are sound in form, but no single small body could be relied upon for their soundness in substance. I have already indicated what I think the proper method of framing laws should be. It is a method already used occasionally or in part both in Britain and here, but nowhere fully or consistently. Responsibility for legislation must be centered in the cabinet; but the cabinet itself, after indicating its general wishes and policy, must call upon different groups of experts actually to frame the bills: banking experts, for example, would collaborate with drafting experts to frame banking bills, taxation experts would collaborate with drafting experts to frame tax bills, and so on. Yet if the full legislative body is to be free to propose and adopt amendments on the floor of the legislature, all this careful work may go for naught.

To prevent this, it seems to me, the full legislative body should not be able by a mere majority vote to

[1] *Ibid.*, p. 236.

amend any bill on the floor. It should restrict itself, in the first instance, merely to referring a proposed amendment back to the cabinet. The cabinet may, after a short consideration, either accept the amendment, incorporate it in modified form, or reject it. If the amendment is rejected, or is so changed in adoption as not to satisfy the full legislature, the full legislature may then vote again upon it, and if it approves the amendment by, say, a majority of two-thirds, the amendment will be adopted. It would be desirable to apply an even more stringent rule against any amendment proposing to increase an expenditure recommended by the cabinet.[1]

This may seem to some readers an undue restriction on the powers of the full legislature and the granting of excessive powers to the cabinet. But we should remember that, although the cabinet would not be legally obliged to accept amendments proposed by the council, or by one of the standing legislative committees, or even by a small majority of those present in the full legislature, it would actually be under great pressure to give serious consideration to these amendment proposals. For a simple majority of the legislature would in the end be able to reject a cabinet-sponsored bill in its entirety. The cabinet could protect itself from alienating members of the standing committees and of the legislature, and from taking the risk of final defeat of its bill, chiefly by lending

---

[1] "The American system has no such wholesome rule as we have, providing that no expenditure can be proposed except by the Government."—RAMSAY MUIR, *How Britain Is Governed*, p. 231.

a hospitable ear to amendment proposals at the various stages. We have also to remember that the final defeat of an important cabinet-sponsored bill, or even an amendment of it over the cabinet's objection, would be so grave a matter that it might force a resignation of the cabinet. The cabinet, therefore, would not be inclined to treat serious proposals for amendment lightly.

Should the cabinet alone originate bills? Are the minority and the private member to be deprived of this power? I think it desirable, if only for the purpose of provoking public discussion and educating public opinion, that the minority members of the council, the standing committees, and private members, should retain the power to introduce bills. But this power should be strictly limited in comparison with its present exercise. There is no good reason, for example, why any private member should be allowed to introduce more than, say, a dozen bills in any one session of the legislature.[1] Not only would this limitation economize on printing and save work for the

[1] In the Seventy-sixth Congress, which began on Jan. 3, 1939, and terminated on Jan. 2, 1941, no fewer than 11,358 bills were introduced (or an average of more than 20 for each member). Of these, 3,113 were reported out by committee, and 1,662 actually became laws. These totals are grossly excessive by any standard. Even if we put aside the 657 private laws, we are left with 1,005 public laws enacted in the session. No single Congressman—indeed, no single human mind—could possibly understand, I shall not say the details, but even the general bearing and effect of more than 1,000 laws passed in two years. Nor is their method of enactment, surely, such as to give any real assurance that each of these laws was properly studied by experts and "must be all right." Under the concentration of responsibility involved in a well-conceived cabinet government, any such reckless and sprawling mass production of laws would be impossible.

member's colleagues; it would make him more careful in the bills that he decided to introduce. It would, in fact, help to protect the member himself from pressure groups.

A private member's bill, when introduced, would be referred to the appropriate standing committee, which would decide upon its fate. If the committee reported the bill favorably by a majority vote, the cabinet would be asked to consider it. If the cabinet rejected it, or took no action within, say, sixty days, the standing committee could vote upon the bill again; and if it favored the bill by a two-thirds vote, it could place the bill before the full House, which could adopt it, say, by a three-fifths vote of those present or an absolute majority of the whole legislature. Under some such procedure, the passage of private members' bills would be rare but not impossible—which is the most desirable situation.

All this would not unduly restrict the power of the individual member of the legislature. "The proper office of a representative assembly," as Mill has declared, "is to watch and control the government: to throw the light of publicity on its acts: to compel a full exposition and justification of all of them which any one considers questionable; to censure them if found condemnable, and, if the men who compose the government abuse their trust, or fulfill it in a manner which conflicts with the deliberate sense of the nation, to expel them from office, and either expressly or virtually appoint their successors." "This," as Mill added, "is surely ample power, and security enough for the liberty of the nation."[1]

5

Before we leave the subject of the legislature, some further points should be made about its structure, its method of election, and its functions. I indicated earlier that cabinet government can be made just as "strong" and as "stable" as we think it wise to make it. It is often said, for example, that the presidential form has more "stability" than the cabinet form of government. When this contention is examined closely, it turns out merely to mean that constitutionally there is no way of forcing the resignation of the executive before the end of a four-year term, and no way of dissolving Congress before the termination of the respective set terms of the Representatives and Senators.

But is this a desirable situation? If it were, the cabinet form of government could achieve it easily enough. The constitution could prescribe that after the legislature met it should elect a premier, but that once having done so, it could not constitutionally change its premier—either for some set period, such as a minimum of a year, or for the whole life of that legislature, say four years. The constitution could also provide that the premier would have no power of dissolving the legislature for a similar period, or perhaps no power of dissolving it at all. We should then have the only kind of "stability" that the presi-

[1] *Representative Government* (Everyman ed.), p. 239.

dential system provides, plus one great merit that the presidential system does not have. The executive would be, at least at the beginning (and possibly throughout), the real choice of the legislature. Therefore the executive and legislature would at least begin by united policy and united action. They could not possibly, for example, be of opposite parties. The executive would be, at least at the beginning, a man whom the majority of the legislature strongly admired. Under the presidential system both difference in party and personal animosity may exist between the executive and the legislative majority from the very beginning.

Would there be any particular advantage, however, in having a cabinet system that was frozen into this kind of "stability"? Suppose that a fundamental difference in policy developed in time between the premier and the parliamentary majority? If the parliament could not force the premier to resign, and the premier could not dissolve the parliament and have the dispute settled by the people at a new election, the premier and the parliament would simply have to continue with this difference in policy. We should then have the kind of recrimination and deadlock so frequent under the presidential system: the premier could not force the parliament to adopt the policy he favored; the parliament might possibly pass laws that he opposed, but they would have to depend upon him for putting them into effect. This is not "stability"; it is the false appearance of stability to cover the reality of paralysis and division. This is all that the vaunted "stability" of the presidential system amounts to—unless the problem is solved, as it usually is in Latin America, by outright presidential dictatorship.

Nothing is to be gained under a cabinet system, in short, by placing any arbitrary constitutional minimum on the term of the premier or the parliament. We must depend upon the common sense of the parliamentary members, upon the premier's power to threaten dissolution, and upon the penalties that the voters will inflict at the polls on anyone who forces them there for what they feel to be trivial or indefensible reasons.

Certain legitimate devices can be adopted, however, to increase the real stability of cabinet government. One of these has to do with the balance of parties in the legislature. As we saw in the examples of Germany and Italy, and as, indeed, Walter Bagehot pointed out seventy-five years ago, before the plan had even been put in operation anywhere, proportional representation is "inconsistent with . . . the conditions which . . . are essential to the bare possibility of parliamentary government." [1] One of the defects of P.R. is that it makes a fetish of a supposed mathematical justice or exactitude. But so, also, in their way, do older democratic techniques. If a political party, for example, wins just 51 per cent of the seats in the legislature, it is the almost universal practice to hold it to that figure, even though this necessarily means a government in a highly unstable equilibrium. One remedy for this condition, which I have

[1] *The English Constitution,* p. 140.

already indicated, is to allow the premier, once chosen, to appoint to his cabinet, if he desires, men who were not elected members of the legislature. They should be granted a vote in the legislature and the cabinet after they have been chosen by the premier and accepted by the legislature. This privilege should exist no matter how large the premier's legislative majority already is. It is, however, a privilege that should be restricted, either directly or by a constitutional limit on the size of the cabinet.

In any event, such a privilege, even if used in an extreme form that is very unlikely, would not add at most more than ten or a dozen votes to the parliamentary majority. Special provision, it seems to me, should be made where a party majority would otherwise be a very narrow one. It could be provided, for example, that any party that had won more than 50 per cent but less than 55 per cent of the seats in the legislature should have the privilege of appointing representatives at large to bring its majority up to 55 per cent of the original legislature. Thus if a party won 51 seats in a legislature of 100 members, it would have the privilege of appointing four additional members, whether or not these were appointed to the cabinet. This would increase the total membership of the legislature slightly, as well as that of the majority party, but this would not be a matter of much practical importance. It might also be provided that the leading party, in any majority existing only through coalition, could add, say, 10 per cent to the number of seats it held, by appointing representatives at large.

Such a device would make for more stable governments wherever a multiparty instead of a two-party system did come into existence in the legislature.

In another way, also, parliamentary government could escape from the fetish of precise arithmetical results. In Europe, cabinets have been known to fall because some government bill or amendment was defeated by a few votes when some of the majority members were out to lunch, or away for the week end. This is an absurd subservience to mathematical accident. In all such cases the premier should have, say, at least a forty-eight-hour veto on the action of the legislature. During that time he should have the opportunity to explain to the legislature and the country the case for the government's measure, as well as the opportunity to round up the government members for a second vote. If defeated a second time, he should be obliged to accept the result. But no government should be forced to resign because of a merely accidental defeat.

In still another way we can make democratic institutions work better by not making a fetish of mathematical results when it is clearly not in the interests of good government to do so. If two parties are very evenly balanced in the total popular vote, they tend (in the absence of gerrymandering) to be evenly balanced in the legislature. A small but definite popular majority, however, often tends, under the orthodox single-member-for-each-district voting system, to become a very large majority in the legislature. Within certain limits, this result is actually desirable, for it

A RESPONSIBLE GOVERNMENT IN OUTLINE: II

makes possible strong and stable government. But the result becomes much less desirable when one party tends to achieve an actual monopoly in the legislature. The advocates of proportional representation make much of the evils of such a result. Thus they point out, to cite but one example, that in the election for the old board of aldermen in New York City, the Democrats in 1935 polled only 66 per cent of the vote but received 95 per cent of the seats, whereas the Republicans, though they polled 26 per cent of the votes, received less than 5 per cent of the seats.[1]

This is the sort of result that the single-member-district system does not have to accept. We can provide simple remedies. We can provide, say, that if a single party gains 75 per cent or more of the seats in a legislature but does not poll an equal percentage of the total vote, then minority parties shall have the privilege of appointing representatives at large to seats in the legislative body sufficient to bring their representation up to 25 per cent of the total of the legislative body so enlarged. The seats at large so added could be divided among the minority parties in proportion to the total popular vote that each of the minority parties had received in the election. No individual minority party, however, nor all the minority parties together, should be allowed representatives at large sufficient to bring their total representation *above* the proportion of the total vote that they had received.

[1] *Cf.* G. H. HALLETT and C. G. HOAG, *Proportional Representation —The Key to Democracy* (1937), p. 19.

One illustration may be cited to show how this would work. Suppose, in a given election, that the leading party polled 60 per cent of the total vote; the second party, 30 per cent; and the third, 10 per cent. Suppose that, in a legislature consisting of 100 seats, this resulted in the first party securing 85 of the seats; the second, 14; and the third, 1. The legislature would thereupon be enlarged to 113 seats, to reduce the leading party to 75 per cent of the total number. The 28 remaining seats would be distributed in the ratio of three-fourths to the second party and one-fourth to the third, to correspond with their respective percentages of the popular vote. But the second party has already won 14 seats and the third party 1. Therefore the second party would be entitled to appoint 7 representatives at large and the third party 6, bringing their total representation to 21 and 7, respectively.

Doubtless the advocates of proportional representation will assert that such a plan is merely stealing their thunder, and that if we are willing to apply their plan to this extent the only logical course is to apply it fully. But there is a vitally important difference between the sort of plan that I have just outlined, and complete P.R. It is not the defect but the virtue of P.R. that it gives minority parties a *voice*. Its fatal defect is that it makes it impossible to secure a solid and enduring majority, and that it enables minorities to obstruct action. Its fatal defect, in short, is that it makes it impossible for a legislature to govern.

Now the sort of plan that I have just suggested

would come into operation only in those places or periods where a single party would otherwise enjoy almost a monopoly in government. This plan would leave that single party strong enough to carry through any reasonable legislative program that it wished; but it would allow other and influential voices to be heard. It would prevent any single party, or any political machine, from achieving a complete monopoly in the legislature unless it could achieve it in the popular vote. For their representatives at large, the minority parties would be likely to choose their ablest and most persuasive advocates. They would thus tend to break up any stagnant one-party monopoly. Dissident voices would be heard at the times when it was most important and least harmful to hear them. But once minority parties had secured a fourth of the seats, they would have to depend upon the customary method of counting returns to increase their legislative representation. They would not be in a position to upset governments or to paralyze action.

Thus, through the utilization of some comparatively simple devices, we could guard against the evils of majority weakness on the one hand or of one-party monopoly on the other.

6

A word should be said at this point about the devices known as the Initiative, Referendum and Recall. The first two, I think, must be rejected, except for extremely limited uses. The basic assumption of representative government is that public questions are complex, and need the special study of persons whose full-time duty it is to give them that study. The average voter has not the time to study the merits of complicated political questions, even if he is assumed to have the ability. It is unfair to ask him to give an answer to some merely general question, such as Do you favor a protective tariff? or Do you favor a program of work relief? unless he knows how this answer is going to be interpreted in particular schedules or in the details of administration. If, on the other hand, a specific measure is prepared and he is asked whether he favors it or not, he is placed in a position where he cannot make reservations. Either he must reject a measure because it contains particular clauses that he does not like, or he must accept it with those clauses; and experience shows that a measure once accepted by referendum acquires so sacrosanct a quality that no legislature dares to touch it with its profane hands, even to make the most obviously necessary amendments. Moreover, once legislators are granted the device of the referendum, they use it to dodge, and to pass on to the voters, every embarrassing issue that arises. Thus they lose the habit of responsibility; they lose the need for courage; and the ultimate effect must be to lower the quality of the legislature.

The only sound use for the referendum is in the adoption of constitutional amendments, for no legislature can be safely depended upon to decide the limits of its own power and authority.

The initiative is a device of even more limited application. It leads to the presentation to the voters of bills that have gone through none of the process of discussion and refinement that a bill goes through in a cabinet or in legislative committees and legislative debate. These initiative bills are usually drawn up by inexperienced reformers or outright cranks.

There is, however, one possible use for the initiative, with all its defects. This is in the presentation to the voters of proposed constitutional amendments *reducing* the powers, terms or numbers of legislators or changing their method of election. For this is the sort of amendment that legislators can never be got to initiate themselves. It is of no avail to be able to change particular legislators when they remain as a class unanimous in defending their established prerogatives. Not a little of the cynicism of the French people about all politicians and about democracy was the result of their feeling of powerlessness to curb the growth and irresponsibility of their parliament and of their whole bureaucracy. This is a peculiarly difficult problem; but some form of safeguarded initiative to meet it might possibly be devised.

On the whole, however, whatever merits the initiative and referendum have for general use (as well as some of their evils and dangers) are already represented in the informal and unofficial "sampling" of the Gallup poll.[1]

The case for a limited form of recall rests on much sounder ground. A man should not be his own doctor

[1] See LINDSAY ROGERS, "Do the Gallup Polls Measure Opinion?" *Harper's Magazine* (November, 1941).

or his own lawyer. But he must be competent enough to choose his doctor and his lawyer. And if he is considered competent to choose them, then he must also be considered competent to change them. He should not be forced to keep them for a period of years, no matter how they turn out; he should be able to change as soon as he has strong reason to become dissatisfied with his original choice. The recall, unlike the initiative and referendum, is a logical corollary of representative government.

The difficulty with it is a technical one, not one of principle. The legislator, unlike the doctor or lawyer, serves a many-headed monster. He cannot hope to please all his constituents; some of them voted against him at the start, and most of these will continue to be against him. If the opposition party, therefore, can start a petition for recall at any time, the representative must live constantly under a sword of Damocles. How can he be expected to act with independence and courage under such conditions?

This problem can be solved, I suggest, by several safeguards. The present term of a member of the House of Representatives is two years. The basic legislative term should be extended to four years. This would answer the present just criticism that we now remove our Congressmen as soon as they have begun to learn their jobs. It could next be provided that no legislator could be subject to the recall until he had served at least six months of his term. It could be further provided that in the event of a recall petition he should be entitled to a certain sum from the

Federal Government to conduct his campaign to remain in office. It could be still further provided that he could not be removed upon a mere majority vote, but only upon a vote against him of, say, at least 52 per cent of the voters. (The purpose of this provision would be to protect chiefly those incumbents who had been elected originally by very narrow majorities, and whose opponents might be tempted to have another try at it.) It could be provided, finally—and this, next to the lengthening of the basic term, I think the most important safeguard—that no representative could be twice put in jeopardy of his office during any single term. In other words, if a representative had to face a recall election at the end of his first year, and won, he would be immune from any such petition for the next three years. Similarly, if a new representative were elected at a recall election, the new representative would also be safe for the balance of the term.

The best method of conducting a recall election, I think, would be to ask the voters to vote at the same election on the recall of the incumbent and for his successor, but to do so on separate ballots. If the incumbent did not receive a negative vote of more than 52 per cent of all the ballots cast with regard to him, he would remain in office, and the balloting on possible successors would be void. If, on the contrary, the incumbent did receive more than a 52 per cent negative vote, but nevertheless if in the succeeding ballot—either because there were more than two candidates or for other reasons—he received a plurality of all the votes cast, or won in accordance with the voting plan proposed in the next chapter, he would be "recalled" and "reelected" at the same election, and would continue in office. This last result seems to me highly improbable. But if it should ever come about, the incumbent, surely, should benefit when the voters cannot agree on anyone whom they want more than him.

Let us see what this recall device would accomplish. It would be unlikely to reduce the ability or the independence of the individual legislator. On the contrary, he would serve normally for a term of four years instead of two. He would not face the certainty of a new election at the end of two years. At the very most, he would be subject to two elections in four years, as now; but these would be likely to occur in only a small number of districts instead of in all; for it would require determined initiative on the part of the voters, positive and active dislike of the legislator, to bring about the recall petition.

Experience shows, indeed, that the recall is a device of rare use even when it is not surrounded by special safeguards.[1] Nevertheless, it is a device of great importance. For it means that the voters can act on a legislator at any time. They can remove him if he becomes involved in a nasty scandal, though the nature of the scandal or the proof may be such that he cannot be impeached or jailed. They do not in such a case have to lie in wait for him for years, while he continues to misrepresent them and while their mem-

[1] *Cf.* "Recall," *Encyclopaedia of the Social Sciences.*

ory of his misconduct has a chance to grow dim. The voters have the same opportunity for removal if their representative's vote upon a crucial measure is such as to anger them particularly.

The recall, finally, if used in connection with a longer basic term, at the same time that it meant fewer elections would provide greater responsiveness and responsibility in the legislature. The people would be able to change legislators at precisely those times when they were most moved to do so.

We have seen that one of the great advantages of the cabinet over the presidential system is its greater flexibility and responsiveness to the public will. The premier can dissolve the legislature and call an election whenever the legislature refuses to follow his leadership. But even such election appeals, though much more flexible than those in a presidential government, are made only when a serious disagreement arises *within* the governmental majority itself. If party discipline keeps a strong legislative majority in line, on the other hand, the people may not get an opportunity to express any disapproval they may feel toward the cabinet's policy. This opportunity arises normally only by the accident of death or forced retirement and a consequent by-election. The recall, on the other hand, enables the voters of a district to hold a by-election on their *own decision* that such an election is necessary. At the same time, under the limitations that I have suggested, the recall privilege could not be abused. But it would supply an instantly applicable test of changes in public sentiment. It would mean more frequent by-elections. And in a crisis, public opinion on its own initiative would be assured a way of making itself decisively felt.

VIII

A RESPONSIBLE GOVERNMENT IN OUTLINE: III

SO FAR, in speaking of "the full legislature," I have had in mind simply a single house. Do we need a second house? I do not believe that the usual reasons put forward in favor of a second house are convincing ones. It is not needed to prevent hasty action and force mature consideration of measures. All this can be done adequately, as we have just seen, by the proper *internal organization* of a single house. The most important single measure in this respect is to centralize responsibility in a small cabinet selected in effect as a general committee of the house. We have seen further that a bill may be put through a number of critical stages in a single house before final adoption. A second house, with power to nullify the decisions of the first, would, with a properly organized first house, do little to secure more mature consideration, and might have precisely the opposite effect. When a house knows that its own decisions are final, its sense of responsibility will usually make it very careful; but if it acts in the knowledge that all its work may go for nothing, it may not take the trouble. A second house tends, in short, by its very existence to make a first house less responsible. The second house itself is less responsible, for the same reason, when its decisions can be rejected by the first. The very situation created by the two-house legislature is then pointed to as proving the need for retaining the two houses!

A two-house legislature is less responsible, also, when each house has equal powers, because it becomes impossible for the public to know where to place responsibility. The Senate, for example, may fail to act on a bill passed overwhelmingly by the House of Representatives, because a single committee chairman in the Senate does not like the bill and refuses to report it out. Legislation to curb a serious evil may fail altogether because the House and Senate cannot agree on the remedy. The public is confused by such technicalities, and does not know whom to hold responsible for the result.

The one arrangement, in brief, that is utterly indefensible is precisely the one we have adopted in our Federal Government and in virtually all our States— a two-house legislature, in which the houses enjoy practically equal powers. In no case should a second house be able to place an absolute veto on the action of the first. A second house, where it exists, should be at most a delaying and revising chamber.

There is little point, further, in the existence of a second house chosen in essentially the same way as the first. Granting that a check is needed, a popularly elected first house is unlikely to receive the proper kind of check from a popularly elected second house.

A directly elected second chamber, moreover, will not be content to remain in an essentially subordinate capacity. It is bound to use the prestige of its direct election to extend its obstructive powers.

We can, however, carry the case against any sort of second house too far. Mr. Laski, for example, attempts to dispose of the problem much too facilely when he argues: "Broadly speaking, any second chamber which agrees with the first is superfluous; and, if it disagrees, it is bound to be obnoxious." [1] One could extend this logic to successive reductions in the membership even of a single chamber until one got down to a single dictator. Mr. Laski's logic, indeed, is precisely that which was once used to condemn the existence of any other book but the Koran: if it agreed with the Koran it was superfluous, and if it disagreed it was bound to be obnoxious.

To reject Mr. Laski's maxim is not, however, to reject the general maxim of Bagehot that "In politics, whatever is unnecessary is pernicious." But there is a real and a highly important function that a properly constituted second chamber can perform. Though it is essential to the democratic process that ultimate power be placed in the hands of a chamber popularly elected, such a chamber has one great weakness. Not only will it enact what it believes to be the popular will of the moment, but it will not even dare to criticize what it believes to be popular will of the moment. Nor will it be content with mere silence. The majority of legislators, on the contrary, will hasten to

[1] *A Grammar of Politics*, p. 331.

adopt the supposed popular opinion as their own. They will end by stating it with much more emphasis than most of the people who originally held it, and with fewer qualifications; for this, they imagine, is the safest route to reelection.

If this is considered an exaggerated picture, or a situation confined to the lower orders of politicians, I need merely cite the extraordinary confession of former Prime Minister Baldwin of Great Britain. We now know that before Hitler invaded Poland, and to an even greater extent before Munich, the democracies were shockingly uninformed. They did not remotely realize either the terrific preparations for war that the Nazis were making or their own governments' appalling lack of preparations. Men who were the titular leaders of the democracies, instead of dealing candidly with their people, instead of impressing their people with the facts that they themselves had learned or were in a position to learn, were in fact followers: they expressed before the voters merely the opinions and sentiments that they believed the voters already to hold. "Supposing," Mr. Baldwin once put the matter with unintended candor, "that I had gone to the country and said that Germany was rearming and that we must rearm, does anybody think that this pacific democracy would have rallied to that cry at that moment? I cannot think of anything that would have made *the loss of the election* from my point of view more certain." (My italics.)

The result of this fear of losing the election, in brief, is that politicians who depend directly upon the popular vote do not have the courage to take positions or to point to truths which they believe to be unpalatable or unpopular. The result is that the case for the assumed unpopular side of a question is often not even presented, and certainly not in a way to force the elected politicians to meet it.

It is of the utmost importance that somewhere, at least, in the government, in a position to wield real influence, there should be a group of statesmen *with the power to tell the people the truth* as they see it. They are likely to do this consistently, I suggest, only if the office that they hold is non-elective, and if, also, they are not removable at the will of those who hold elective office. The one place where such a group of statesmen could properly function would be in a second chamber, which would have the power, not indeed to nullify or indefinitely to obstruct legislation passed by the first chamber, but to criticize it, to delay it, to revise it; above all, to force the first chamber to reconsider it.

The ideal house for this function would be a small one, the members of which were chosen by the first house. Probably the best method for this choice would be by an election in the first house under proportional representation. This second house need not consist of more than, say, two dozen members. The individual terms of the members might be equal to two terms in the lower house. Their terms could overlap, like those in the present Senate, with one-half of the members of the second house being chosen by each new lower house. The members of the upper house so chosen would probably be men who had occupied prominent public positions in the nation, and who commanded wide national respect. It would be a way of utilizing the ability and experience of men who for one reason or another did not care to put themselves forward for election to office but would accept such an appointment.

Such a second house, I suggest, should not have the power of holding up bills passed by the first house for more than thirty or sixty days. At the end of such a period, if the second house failed to take action, a bill would automatically become law. But the second house could propose amendments to a bill or reject it wholly. In either case, the bill would return to the first house. The first house would consider the amendments and perhaps appoint a conference committee to decide which should be adopted. If the first house wished to reject the amendments, however, or to re-pass a rejected bill, it would have to re-pass it, say, either by a three-fifths vote or by an absolute majority of the whole membership. If it failed to do so, it would have to wait for at least six months from the rejection of the bill by the second house before it could re-pass it by an ordinary majority. In the meanwhile, perhaps, the effect on public opinion of the debates in the second house, or a change in conditions, might be such that the bill would not again receive a majority in the first house.

A second house of this type, with these limited powers, would not be able to obstruct or thwart any policy strongly desired by the nation or by a sufficient majority in the first house; but it would be able to force the first house to reconsider, and it would be able to deal candidly with the public and to tell it truths that the first house would hesitate to tell. In this way it would keep public opinion more healthy than it is likely to be when there is no one in the government who dares to call it mistaken. To protect the members of the second house from political ambitions that might undermine their courage to perform this particular function, it might be provided that no member of the second house could seek elective office for a period of two years after the end of his term or after his resignation.

I have suggested a small house because only a small house is needed for this function, and because it is desirable that the members have sufficient individual prominence for their opinions to carry weight with the public. It cannot be seriously argued that two dozen men would be too few for this purpose. A not unsimilar function, indeed, is performed today by single individuals. The President and the Governors of the States must pass upon all bills to decide in each case whether or not to veto them. For their decisions, these executives usually depend, or ought to depend, on expert advisers. The proposed second house should also depend for guidance upon expert advisers of its own selection.

2

Up to now, in the last three chapters, I have written in a frankly hypothetical vein. My purpose has been to ask what sort of political institutions would be most desirable, apart from the likelihood of our being able to get them. I have done this because I have reserved later chapters to discuss practical compromises. But we must be at least realistic enough to recognize that an especially formidable barrier stands in the way of our being able to obtain a second house constituted as I have just suggested. Article V, the amendatory article to the Constitution, makes one exception even to the extremely difficult general method of amendment that it permits. It provides in its final clause that "no State, without its consent, shall be deprived of its equal suffrage in the Senate."

Thus there is embedded in the Constitution one clause that it would be practically impossible to get rid of by any peaceful means whatever. One can understand the original reasons for this provision. At a time when the proposed union was thought of primarily as a federation and not as a nation, it was considered necessary to reassure the small States that they would not be outvoted by their larger neighbors if they joined this federation. Since the discrepancies among the thirteen original States were not excessive, the provision doubtless seemed reasonable at the time.

But it now protects a fantastic rotten-borough system, and so far as one can see it protects it *forever*. Since the original union, new States have been admitted which were largely artificial creations—including great tracts of land without people—and which needed no such assurance. The two Senators from New York represent *one hundred twenty-five times* as many people as the two Senators from Nevada; yet they are reduced to the same vote in the Senate. A majority of the national population in 1930 was in the sixteen States of the industrial Northeast, but these States were represented by only one-third of the members of the Senate. Twelve States in the prairie and mountain regions had altogether only three-fourths of the population of New York State; yet New York's population of 12,500,000 had altogether only two votes in the Senate, whereas the 8,300,000 people in these twelve States had twenty-four votes in the Senate. This has given the rural and farming areas of the country a gross over-representation in the Senate.[1] If they had used this only to prevent incursions on an agreed domain of their own state sovereignty, it would be one thing. They have used their gross over-representation, in fact, however, to vote for all sorts of spending schemes to benefit their own States disproportionately, and to saddle the cost upon the more populous parts of the country. (It would be instructive to study this situation in connection with the fantastic silver-purchase acts of recent years, as one example.)

Yet, assuming that the overwhelming majority of the country finally decided that this plan of representation was a vicious one, what could be done to get rid of it? If even one State objects, it can permanently block such a change. And it is inconceivable that the Nevadas and Dakotas and Wyomings would ever willingly relinquish the huge advantage they

[1] *Cf.* Arthur C. Millspaugh, *Democracy, Efficiency, Stability* (1942), p. 302.

derive from their equality of voting power in the Senate with New York, Illinois and Pennsylvania. This is America's form of the "Polish veto." [1]

It has been suggested that it would be "immoral" ever to try to change this clause in our Constitution either by the process prescribed for all other amendments or even by a new constitutional convention, unless this impossible unanimous consent of every State could be obtained. It may be pertinent to consider the ethics of ever inserting a clause like this in the first place. If we cannot change it now, after a lapse of a century and a half, without unanimous consent, the same reasons will prevent us from changing it after another century and a half, or even a thousand years from now. For how long do the framers of a constitution or other document have a moral right to bind future majorities among their successors? Surely there should be a moral statute of limitations

---

[1] This astonishing institution existed in Poland in the seventeenth century and through most of the eighteenth, until 1791. Its working is thus described in the *Encyclopaedia Britannica*, Vol. 18, p. 142: "The *liberum veto* was based on the assumption of the absolute political equality of every Polish gentleman, with the corollary that every measure introduced into the Polish diet must be adopted unanimously. Consequently, if any single deputy believed that a measure already approved by the rest of the house might be injurious to his constituency, he had the right to exclaim *nie pozwalam,* 'I disapprove,' when the measure fell at once to the ground. Subsequently this vicious principle was extended still further. A deputy, by interposing his individual veto, could at any time dissolve the diet, when all measures previously passed had to be resubmitted to the consideration of the following diet. Before the end of the seventeenth century the *liberum veto* was used so recklessly that all business was frequently brought to a standstill. Later it became the chief instrument of foreign ambassadors for dissolving inconvenient diets, as a deputy could always be bribed to exercise his veto."

running not longer than the traditional ninety-nine-year lease!

However we may answer this question in political philosophy, we shall doubtless, as a practical matter, have to accept the permanent equality of state representation in the Senate. This debars us from the sort of second house, chosen by the first, outlined above as probably the most satisfactory form of second house. It debars us as well from the consideration of many other possible ways of forming a second chamber. Fortunately, however, nothing in the Constitution declares that the Senate must always have the same powers, absolutely or relatively to the House, as it has in the original Constitution. If there were such a clause, the introduction of any genuine reform in our Constitution, giving us an efficient cabinet government, would be forever impossible.

For years Americans obscurely realized that there was something wrong in the working of Congress. But they made the wrong diagnosis, and so adopted the wrong remedy. It was true that there was something inherently undemocratic about a second chamber, indirectly elected, exercising equal and coordinate powers with a chamber directly chosen by the people. But the evil was not, as they falsely concluded at the time, that the second chamber was indirectly elected. The real evil was that it had equal powers with the first. Yet they changed its method of election to direct election, while retaining its equal powers with the House. By doing this they created a second popularly elected House, which is unnecessary, and they allowed it to retain the power to nullify absolutely the decisions of the first House, which is pernicious. Clearly they should have retained the indirect election of the Senate, but removed its power to nullify the legislation of the House or the treaties of the executive. They should have made the Senate, in brief, a mere delaying and revising chamber, with the limited powers for such a chamber outlined a few pages back.

It is commonly said that the choice of Senators by state legislatures was abandoned because it led to corruption. I am unable to find any logic in the view that directly elected legislators are honest but that the legislators which *they* in turn choose are corrupt. If the directly elected state legislators made corrupt choices, it was because they themselves were corrupt; if they were honest, they made honest choices. The question of corruption is largely irrelevant to that of direct or indirect election. Opportunities for corruption are likely to occur only when Senators are chosen by legislatures in an anonymous manner that makes it difficult to fix responsibility for the choice. If they were chosen by public nominations in the two Houses of the state legislature meeting in joint session, and by secret ballot participated in by all members, with the final result confirmed by public ballot, responsibility for the choice could be properly fixed on particular members of the state legislature.

With the lessened role that the Senate would play under the plan I have outlined—*i.e.*, the role merely of delaying, revising, forcing the House to reconsider measures, and telling the people unpalatable or unpopular truths—it could safely enough retain the present inelastic system of overlapping six-year terms, which is pernicious only as long as the Senate retains its present power to veto absolutely the action of the House or to thwart the popular will. A Senate with the lessened powers and responsibilities that I have indicated, however, would have no need of ninety-six members. Its quality would be raised if only one instead of two Senators were chosen from each State, and if the residential qualification were removed.

3

I remarked earlier (Chap. VI, Sec. 4) that the traditional "constitutional monarch" is the result less of deliberate contrivance than of historic accident; that it is possible to imagine a cabinet government with no substitute for that monarch in the form of a president; and that where a premier exists, the discretionary powers of a president should be reduced to the minimum. Nevertheless, I believe that there are functions for such a president important enough to justify the existence of the office.

One function of the president would be to symbolize a permanent impartial government above the seesaw and bickerings of party politics. This is one of the chief functions that the English Crown performs: the King symbolizes that permanent government to which every citizen can give his full loyalty. It is true that such a symbol is not indispensable. The President of the United States, for example, is at once the head of the nation and a party leader. But his dual role often causes confusion, particularly around election time: he is able to exploit his role as head of the nation unduly to strengthen his party and his role as party leader. The opposition finds itself in the embarrassing position of having to pledge allegiance to the President as head of the nation while denouncing him as leader of the rival party. It helps to clarify thought, therefore, while it frees party criticism for its proper scope, and prevents it from weakening loyalty to the permanent part of the State itself, if the function of party leader and the function of titular head of the State are performed by two different men with different offices, the premier and the president.

Another function of a president would be to relieve the premier of all routine social and ceremonial duties —the duty of formally receiving ambassadors, of signing commissions and orders, of presenting medals, laying corner stones, unveiling monuments, attending important public dinners, proclaiming holidays, and making the speeches that the head of a State must make. Such a division of labor is especially important in a great country like the United States.

It could be supplemented by a still further division of labor. The premier should have the right to appoint a deputy premier and to delegate to him whatever administrative functions he thinks necessary. Such a deputy might be authorized to sign many routine documents and to make certain appointments in the place of the premier. He should sit in the cabinet, but in order that he should be free for his administrative duties it would seem undesirable for him to be a party leader or a legislative member with a vote in congress or the cabinet. What I have in mind is an official who would be something more than a private secretary to the premier (because of the actual delegation of powers) but something less than a cabinet member, because he would play no role in formulating policy. He would relieve the premier, in other words, of certain *managerial* functions while the president relieved the premier of *ceremonial* functions. The more of his time the premier is free to devote to formulating and effectuating broad policies, the better.

But a president should not be a mere ceremonial figure subordinate to the premier. He is needed on occasion to exercise real discretion and to make important decisions. He should have the power of nominating a premier whenever the verdict of the legislature is not a clear one (though the power of accepting or rejecting the premier so nominated must, of course, remain with the legislature). He may urge a premier not to resign when the circumstances do not seem to require resignation. He should not be given the power to prevent a premier from dissolving the legislature, but he should have the power of threatening to declare publicly, whenever he thought so, that a dissolution was inadvisable or unwarranted. Thus he could mitigate the premier's power of dissolution if it were ever invoked for some trivial reason.

Finally, there may be occasions on which the president would himself have power to dissolve the legislature. If the legislature's regular term happened to end in time of war or other emergency, it might be thought highly undesirable that a general election should be held then. In such a case, following its declaration of an emergency, the legislature might be permitted to continue its term for one or two years upon a two-thirds or three-quarters vote of its members. But the legislature should not be the sole judge of the need to extend its own term. It should have to obtain also the consent of the president, who would have the right to dissolve it, at his discretion, at any time in its self-extended term, and to order an election.

How should the president be elected? For a president with the limited powers of discretion here outlined, the method of popular election, with its nominating conventions, campaign speeches and huge machinery, would be incongruous and altogether unsuited. A president with a direct popular mandate behind him, moreover, would not content himself with these functions. He would feel himself justified in taking a hand in questions of policy. There would then follow all the dangers of a difference in policy between himself and the premier—*i.e.*, between himself and the majority in congress—and we might find ourselves back with the deadlocks and irresponsibility of our present system. It is altogether desirable, therefore, that the president should be elected by both houses of congress sitting jointly. He should be elected for a long term—anywhere from five to ten years—and should be removable only by impeachment.

4

This volume is concerned principally with the reform of the executive and legislative branches of our government. It does not pretend to be a complete treatise on political institutions, and the reform of judicial and administrative agencies, for example, is mainly beyond its scope. It should be obvious, however, that the first step in reforming judicial and administrative institutions is to secure an efficient and responsible legislature and executive with the leisure and intelligence to effect such reform. One reason that our administrative agencies run wild and exercise irresponsible powers is that Congress and the executive, as organized at present, do not have the time either to set up such agencies properly in the first place or to supervise them properly later. Today a favorite resort of Congress' is to throw into the lap of an administrative agency a problem that it does not have either the time, the intelligence or the courage to solve for itself. Later, Congressmen express a sort of hopeless indignation at the manner in which the administrative agency that they have set up is dealing with the question.

The central problem concerning the administrative agencies is how to protect the rights of citizens, and to keep the bureaucracy from getting out of bounds, without hampering its practical action excessively by court vetoes and other legal restrictions. A few reasonably obvious rules and practices suggest themselves:

1. To begin with, Congress should delegate power very carefully and precisely.

2. Discretion for an administrative agency should be granted only to the extent necessary. The law should be as "automatic" as possible—*i.e.*, nothing should be left to a commission's discretion that might reasonably be incorporated in the law itself. This will enable citizens to know as clearly as possible the extent of their rights and duties, and will restrict the possible realm of administrative discrimination or caprice.

3. To supplement the customary annual recommendations to Congress of a governmental commission (which are almost invariably pleas for more funds, more personnel or more power), Congress should appoint an "advisory commission" covering the same ground. The members of the latter body should be distinguished private citizens, expert in the field, who would serve without pay. Their function should be to follow the work of the commission (for which they might be allotted at least one single full-time secretary with pay), and to make recommendations to the commission and to Congress regarding the commission's powers. This advisory commission would serve as Congress's and the people's watch-dog on that particular commission. The advisory commission would presumably praise where praise was due, but also criticize any unsound or dangerous tendencies of the commission. Democracy should be made, as far as possible, continuously *self-criticizing* in nature. Advisory commissions would be an important step

in this direction. They would perform somewhat the same function for each commission (though their powers would be purely recommendatory) that a properly chosen but subordinate second house in the legislature does for the first house: they would be in a continuous position to draw public attention to excesses. It is true that this function is performed for the administrative agencies in part by Congress and the press; but the function would be performed much more adequately if there existed quasi-official bodies whose special duty it was to perform it.

4. Each administrative commission should be obliged to report to the appropriate standing committee in Congress all the rulings of a general nature that it makes during a year. The standing Congressional committee (though it has itself only advisory powers) should privately or publicly warn the commission against any rulings that it thinks unjustified, and should decide whether or not to recommend to Congress that certain of the other rulings be incorporated in the law itself.

5. Because of the tendency of bureaucracy to grow and grow, no commission should be granted a life of more than twenty-five years at most. It should have to be renewed by positive legislation after that, preferably after study of its work by some expert committee especially appointed for the purpose.

5

We have now covered the essential outlines, even down to matters of detail, of what a truly responsible democratic government would be like if we could secure it. There is some danger to my chief contentions, I recognize, in having gone into these details. "Political science," or at least that branch of it which involves devising governmental techniques or supposedly ideal systems, is unfortunately *not* a science—though it should, of course, be approached as far as possible in a scientific spirit. It is essentially an art—an affair rather of balanced judgment and common sense than of either mere ingenuity or immutable law. A device ideally adapted to one people at one time may be badly adapted to another people or another time. (Unfortunately this truth is often perverted into the idiotic dogma that the ideal political institutions for any people are *precisely those they already happen to have*, and that any change would be dangerous.)

Because the suitability of political institutions is so much a matter of judgment and reasonable presumption rather than of scientific proof, I can hardly hope that any reader will agree with every position I have taken or with every proposal I have made. In proportion as one goes into detail in these matters, one courts disagreement. But I hope that the reader will not allow his disagreement with me on this or that point to prejudice him against my main thesis. As I indicated at the beginning, it is often only by considering details that we can be sure our minds are clear regarding general principles. In all the specific proposals I have made, I have tried to keep steadily in mind the political ideal formulated by Bentham and Mill—"the combination of complete popular control over public affairs, with the greatest attainable perfection of skilled agency."[1]

As I remarked a few pages back, this volume makes no attempt to be a comprehensive treatise on political principles: its main and almost sole concern is with the reform of the executive and legislative aspects of our government. Yet it is immediately relevant to this purpose to keep in mind one very broad political principle. The greatest internal threat to parliamentary government today is the excessive interventionism of nearly all governments. No one, to my knowledge, has stated this danger more impressively in compact form than the Swedish economist, Gustav Cassel. I cannot do better than to quote his words, which, spoken eight years ago, already seem prophetic:

> The leadership of the State in economic affairs which advocates of Planned Economy want to establish, is, as we have seen, necessarily connected with a bewildering mass of governmental interferences of a steadily cumulative nature. The arbitrariness, the mistakes and the inevitable contradictions of such policy will, as daily experience shows, only strengthen the demand for a more rational co-ordination of the different measures and, therefore, for unified leadership. For this reason Planned Economy will always tend to develop into Dictatorship. . . .
>
> The existence of some sort of parliament is no guaran-

[1] JOHN STUART MILL, *Autobiography* (1873), (World's Classics ed), p. 225.

tee against planned enonomy being developed into dictatorship. On the contrary, experience has shown that representative bodies are unable to fulfill all the multitudinous functions connected with economic leadership without becoming more and more involved in the struggle between competing interests, with the consequence of a moral decay ending in party—if not individual—corruption. Examples of such a degrading development are indeed in many countries accumulating at such a speed as must fill every honorable citizen with the gravest apprehensions as to the future of the representative system. But apart from that, this system cannot possibly be preserved, if parliaments are constantly overworked by having to consider an infinite mass of the most intricate questions relating to private economy. *The parliamentary system can be saved only by wise and deliberate restriction of the functions of parliaments.* (My italics.)

At the same time, in brief, that we must increase the efficiency of democratic government for carrying on the tasks that it cannot escape, we must reduce the tasks that we impose on democratic government, lest it be forced to change its whole nature to achieve them. Professor Cassel continues with consideration of an even broader question that is still more outside the immediate scope of this volume, but which is of such vital importance that I cannot forebear quoting it:

Economic dictatorship is much more dangerous than people believe. Once authoritative control has been established it will not always be possible to limit it to the economic domain. If we allow economic freedom and self-reliance to be destroyed, the powers standing for Liberty will have lost so much in strength that they will not be able to offer any effective resistance against a progressive extension of such destruction to constitutional and public life generally. And if this resistance is gradually given up—perhaps without people ever realizing what is actually going on—such fundamental values as personal liberty, freedom of thought and speech and independence of science are exposed to imminent danger. What stands to be lost is nothing less than the whole of that civilization that we have inherited from generations which once fought hard to lay its foundations and even gave their life for it.[1]

[1] GUSTAV CASSEL, "From Protectionism through Planned Economy to Dictatorship," Sixth Richard Cobden Lecture, published as a pamphlet (1934).

IX

A BETTER VOTING METHOD

IT IS astonishing how crudely designed the machinery of democracy often is to achieve its basic purposes. The orthodox system of election presumably exists to choose candidates who most nearly represent the sentiments of the voters or have the approval of most of them. But this end is often thwarted by the election system itself.

This is particularly true when more than two candidates are running for the same office. Let us suppose, to take the simplest example, that the race is between Black, White and Gray. Black, we shall say, is an extremist of the right; White, an extremist of the left; Gray, a moderate. The preference of many voters is Mr. Gray. But their greatest fear is the election of Mr. Black. They are told that the real race is between Black and White, and that a vote for Gray is therefore in effect half a vote for Black. Shall they "waste" their votes on Gray, who is least likely to be elected, or waste them on White, whom they do not quite want to see elected, but who is at any rate not Black? This is a typical voter's dilemma in a three- or many-cornered race. Must he pass by his first choice and vote instead for his second or third choice in order to prevent the election of the candidate he most fears?

The prevailing election practice is to declare the winner to be whichever candidate receives the largest number of votes, regardless of whether or not he is the choice of a majority of the voters. To see just how badly such a system can sometimes work, take as an example the special election for United States Senator held in Texas on June 28, 1941. The official returns revealed no fewer than twenty-nine candidates running for that one office. Twenty-five were Democrats. A total of 575,786 votes was cast. To get on the ballot in Texas must be amazingly easy. Sixteen of the twenty-nine candidates received less than 100 votes each; twenty-four received less than 1,000. If there had been some moderate but effective nuisance penalty, as there surely ought to have been, for any candidate failing to receive as much as 1 per cent of the total vote, or even one-half of 1 per cent, there would have been only four candidates in the race.

This great race was won by Governor W. Lee O'Daniel, with a total of 175,590 votes. He was followed very closely by Lyndon B. Johnson, with 174,279 votes. Gerald Mann was third, with 140,000, and Martin Dies fourth, with 80,000. Mr. O'Daniel, in other words, was elected even though only 30 per cent of the voters expressed a preference for him. For all that the balloting itself revealed, he might have been anathema to 70 per cent of the voters of

Texas. Yet O'Daniel was sent to the Senate to represent them.

Where some attempt is made to prevent the election of a candidate not wanted by a majority of the voters, the device most often resorted to is the second ballot, or run-off election. This is employed in some American States and was used in French parliamentary elections before the 1940 collapse. Under this system, a week or two after the first election the other candidates retire from the field, and (usually) the two candidates that have received most votes in the previous election fight it out between them. This device is cumbersome; it involves needless expense, time and effort; and in many if not most cases there is no good reason to assume even that it achieves its main object.

In the Texas election just cited, for example, the two leading candidates even together polled only 60 per cent of the total vote. There is no conclusive reason for assurance that a run-off election between them would have expressed the real choice of the majority of the voters among all the candidates originally in the race. True, such a run-off election would at least have answered the question concerning which was the more acceptable candidate to the majority as between Mr. O'Daniel and Mr. Johnson, which was more than the first election answered. But it might well be that a really accurate method of determining the voters' choice would have shown that Mr. Mann, who ran third, or Congressman Dies, running fourth, was more acceptable to the majority of the voters than either Mr. O'Daniel or Mr. Johnson.

A BETTER VOTING METHOD

Efforts have been made, though seldom applied in large popular elections, to devise a genuinely scientific method of determining the voters' real choice in this matter. These methods have failed to meet with acceptance for two main reasons: either they are too complicated to appeal to or be understood by the average voter, or they may fail no less than cruder methods to reflect the voters' real choice.

The second objection applies to the simplest of these methods, the Bucklin system, first used in Grand Junction, Colo. Under this the voter marks his "first choice," "second choice" and "other choices." If no candidate has an absolute majority of first choices, second choices are counted. If any candidate has a majority of the electors voting, by adding together first and second choices, he is declared elected. If more than one candidate has a majority, the one having the highest number of votes is declared elected. If no candidate has a majority of all the electors voting when second choices are counted, then "other choices" are counted. Whether or not any candidate then has a majority of all the electors voting, the candidate with the highest number of votes is declared elected.

It should be clear that this system could do more harm than good, so far as helping the voters to elect their real choice is concerned. Suppose that the Texas Senatorial election just cited had been conducted according to this system. It is possible that no candidate would have been voted for by a clear majority of all the electors, even when first and later choices were added. If the voters for O'Daniel, then, had voted for Johnson for second or a later choice, they could easily have defeated their first choice; for Johnson, on the first and later choices added together, might have had more votes than O'Daniel.

In other words, under this system of counting, the voters who indicate a second choice can thereby easily hurt the chances of their first choice. Those who indicate a later choice, again, can just as easily hurt the chances of their second choice. Voters have not been slow to recognize this defect in practice. The result has been that where this particular system has been tried few voters mark any choice beyond the first.

To escape the defects of this method, much more complicated systems of voting and counting have been devised that oblige the voter to number, respectively, his first, second, third, fourth, choices, etc. These are known as the "alternative vote," the "Nanson system," the "Hallett system," etc. Much mathematical ingenuity has gone into them. But they are too complicated for the average voter. They would bewilder him and arouse his suspicions that the decisions were being arrived at in some obscure mathematical way to which he did not possess the key. They greatly increase the possibility of invalid ballots. They involve almost incredible complications in counting. In the Texas election just cited, the alternative vote could easily have required more than twenty separate tabulations to determine the result. Space does not permit a description of these complications here. Those who are interested may consult the able book *Proportional Representation*, by C. G. Hoag and G. H. Hallett, Jr., where (pages 480-508) such systems are sympathetically described. (These majority preferential systems, however, are not to be confused with proportional representation, which has a different purpose.)

To those who object to the time, expense and complications in counting, the answer is sometimes made that these complications concern merely the election officials and not the voter. But the voter wants to know clearly, and is entitled to know clearly, how his vote is counted. Otherwise it is difficult to convince him that making a second choice does not hurt his first choice, or a third choice his second, etc. He is not likely to be satisfied with the answer that "mathematicians have figured the whole thing out," and that his later choices cannot hurt his first choices.

Moreover, it is clear that the alternative vote method of counting in a triangular race might eliminate immediately the very candidate most acceptable to the majority of the voters. If, out of 100 voters, 35 vote for White, a leftist, 34 for Black, a rightist, and 31 for Gray, a middle-of-the-road candidate, Gray would be automatically eliminated after the counting of first choices on the ballots, though second choices might show him to be the only candidate acceptable to a majority of the voters.

A method of voting is possible, I think, that would eliminate the misrepresentation that often occurs under the orthodox single-choice method of voting, at the same time that it would avoid the misrepresentations that can occur under the Bucklin system and the excessive complications of supposedly "exact" preferential voting.

The method is simple. Under it, in any race in which more than two candidates were running for the same office, the voter would, as usual, set down his first choice. But in addition, he would have the privilege of marking any other candidate or candidates who were "acceptable" to him, without indicating any preferences among them.

The counting would also be simple. Any candidate who received more than half of all first choices would, of course, be declared elected. But if no candidate received such a majority, then "acceptables" as well as first choices would be counted. If by the addition of "acceptance" votes to first-choice votes only one candidate were found to be acceptable to a majority of all the voters, he would be declared elected. But if more than one candidate were found to be acceptable to a majority of the voters, then the candidate among these with the largest number of *first* choices would be declared elected, without reference to the exact number of voters to whom he was also "acceptable."

The reason for this method of voting and counting is that under this system we should know two things about the winning candidate which, in combination, ought to be decisive: (1) that he was the first choice of more voters than any other candidate, and (2)

A BETTER VOTING METHOD

that he was also acceptable to a majority of all the voters.

To bring out the advantages of such a method of voting and counting, a few examples may be desirable, proceeding from those obviously most favorable to the method to those apparently least favorable to it. The case most obviously favorable to the method would be that in which the candidate who received the largest number of first choices was also found to be the only one "acceptable" to more than half the voters. Almost as favorable would be the case in which, though more than one candidate was found to be acceptable to more than half the voters, the candidate with the most first choices was also the one with the largest number of first and alternative votes combined.

The next most favorable case would be that in which no candidate at all was voted "acceptable" to a majority of all the voters, but in which the candidate who received the greatest number of first choices was found to be also the candidate with the largest number of first and alternative choices combined. It could be argued, it is true, that the alternative vote here proposed would in this case have revealed little about the voters' preferences beyond what would have been revealed by the orthodox method of voting. But the method would at least have established that there was no compromise candidate more acceptable to a majority of the voters than the candidate receiving the largest number of first choices. This negative information would not be without value.

A NEW CONSTITUTION NOW

We come now to the possible cases that seem at first glance least favorable to the method of voting here proposed. One is that in which another candidate receives more first and alternative votes combined than does the candidate who has received most first choices, and in which, in addition, both candidates are acceptable to more than half the voters. Suppose that there are five candidates, Messrs. White, Black, Gray, Green and Brown, in an election in which a total of 100 voters participate. Let us say the result is as follows:

Candidates	First choice	Acceptable	Total votes received
White	44	21	65
Black	36	11	47
Gray	9	59	68
Green	7	8	15
Brown	4	6	10

Under the Bucklin method of voting and counting, Gray would be declared elected. It is clear, however, that Gray is not wanted by the voters on his own merits but almost wholly as a second-choice compromise. In this case there is no reason for electing Gray when White, who leads on first choices, is also found to be acceptable to a majority of the voters. It is clear that White represents the voters' real choice more nearly than Gray. To elect Gray in such circumstances, even though he has a larger total of alternative votes, would be to give excessive encouragement to compromise candidacies as such—to middle-of-the-

A BETTER VOTING METHOD

roadism or fence straddling for its own sake. It would be to ignore altogether the *intensity* of the voters' desire for a given candidate.

The spirit of compromise, it is true, is essential to the success of democracy. Election methods should not be of a type to discourage this spirit from playing its necessary role. Antagonisms that become too profound or bitter lead to civil war and the displacement of democracy by totalitarianism. (Spain is the clearest —though far from the only—present-day example of this.) It is a merit of the method of voting here proposed that at the same time as it would reflect popular sentiment more fully and accurately than the present prevailing method, it would encourage reasonable compromise in several ways. In a three-or-more-cornered race, it would permit voters to name their first choice with comparatively little risk that in doing so they were helping to elect the candidate they most feared. Naming their real first choice would not prevent them from accepting also another candidate more likely to defeat the one they most disliked. For this reason minority groups would not be forced to under-represent their strength, as they so often are at present.

The system would also give increased opportunities to compromise candidates where the fight would otherwise be merely between two extremists. If the example above were slightly altered, and Gray had been indeed the only candidate "acceptable" to a majority of the voters, even with first choices remaining the same, then one could say for Gray that at least he represented the majority of the voters better than anyone else. On that basis he would be entitled to election; and he would actually be the candidate elected under the plan here proposed.

One warning is important. Voting systems must be judged by the way they are likely to work in the largest number of cases, not by the way they *can* work in some very exceptional case. Under certain circumstances it is no doubt possible for a voter with the system here proposed to hurt the chances of his first choice by naming another candidate "acceptable" to him. But it would be reasonably clear to the voter under what circumstances this would happen. He need not use the privilege of naming other "acceptable" candidates if he does not wish to, in which case he will at least be no worse off than under the existing plurality system. Usually, I think, he *will* wish to use this privilege. He will wish to do so, certainly, whenever he doubts that his first choice has a good chance of election. He will wish to do so whenever he is even more eager (as he often is) to make sure of the defeat of one particular candidate than to make sure of the victory of his own first choice (who may merely seem the least obnoxious of the choices that the ballot offers to him). That voting system is to be preferred which, without excessive complications, most clearly reveals the real wishes of the voters and best effectuates those wishes.

The foregoing plan, which might be called the "majority acceptance" method, has not, to my knowledge, hitherto been used or proposed. Yet it would be far simpler than any other majority preferential system. Its simplicity would keep spoiled ballots to a minimum. It requires at most only two countings of the ballots to determine the result. It is more likely than any other system to reveal the real choice of the voters in any contest for the same office in which more than two candidates appear. It would be particularly useful in direct primary elections. It would save enormous time and tedium (and result in better selections) if adopted also by political party conventions in choosing their candidates.

As a nation we have been unduly slow—perhaps dangerously slow—to adopt improvements in democratic political techniques. We tend to dismiss proposals of this sort somewhat scornfully as improvements in "mere machinery." But—to repeat a comparison I have made earlier—just as we cannot hope to turn out first-rate airplane engines or tanks without first-rate machine tools, so we cannot hope to turn out the best democratic decisions, most nearly representing thoughtful public opinion, unless our political machinery is well rather than badly adapted to achieve this end.

X

MINOR REFORMS

IN THE four preceding chapters I have endeavored to set forth what an ideal constitution and other political institutions might be like if we could start with a clean slate—*i.e.*, if we could start without the accumulated prejudices, the timid conservatism and the powerful vested interests in the existing political system that we actually have. But we are compelled to deal with the situation as we find it. It is the thesis of this volume not only that a parliamentary system would be incomparably more flexible, efficient and responsible than our presidential system, but that the latter has defects which could prove fatal to the country in a crisis like the present one. This means that our Constitution should be revised radically—and *now*. But suppose that the country cannot be brought to see this, or that persons in key positions, in spite of a change in national sentiment, prove powerful enough to block or deflect demands for reform? What then?

If our position must be realistic, it need not be defeatist. I have quoted earlier in this volume the remark of Harold J. Laski that "The case made, over seventy years ago, by Bagehot against the ultimate principles of the presidential system seems to me to have been strengthened, rather than weakened, by time." Yet he immediately continues: "But I doubt whether anything short of actual revolution would cause direct changes of the kind necessary to be made. The power of tradition is too great; the interests that could be mobilized against them are too strong."[1] One will find similar declarations in a score of political writers.

Now despairing comment of this sort easily degenerates, among Americans, into an excuse for constitutional do-nothingism. No doubt many serious students of politics in the United States, if examined closely, will agree that the parliamentary system is preferable —some will admit incomparably preferable—to the presidential. But it is also typical of most of them, unfortunately, to say that the American people cannot be persuaded to change the system; and *therefore the trained political students themselves do not seriously advocate the change.* It is a frequent occurrence to find American books on politics which, somewhere in the preface or introduction, will say parenthetically and apologetically that while basic changes in the Constitution are desirable there is no sentiment for them. They go on to make the tacit assumption that it is a waste of time to talk about such basic changes. The entire volume is then given over to discussion of the possibility of some minor change that leaves the basic evil untouched, or, worse, urges that the Constitution be "interpreted" to mean something else

[1] *The American Presidency*, p. 248.

than it plainly says. Such writers, by their timorous acquiescence in the public opinion that exists, merely help to perpetuate the very constitutional evils they privately deplore. No evil can be reformed unless those who recognize it as an evil have the courage to say so and the energy to convert others to their view. The very reasonableness of cabinet government for America has perhaps worked against its adoption. Those who are convinced of its superiority are not likely to be fanatics or proselytizers by temperament.

I believe, however, that Bryce has come nearer than Mr. Laski to stating the main reason that has stood in the way of constitutional change: *"The process of amending the Constitution is so troublesome* [my italics] that even a change which involves no party issues may remain unadopted long after the best opinion has become unanimous in its favor."[1] Our first point of attack, therefore, should be on the present amending process itself. This point is so important that I shall later devote a special chapter to it.

Because the importance of this change in the amending process itself has never been brought home with sufficient force to the American people, less sentiment exists for it than for other changes that are inherently of much less importance or value. We must utilize, however, whatever sentiment for change already exists, wherever the changes desired are in themselves good.

When we review the minor amendments that are most frequently urged or that seem most desirable

[1] *The American Commonwealth*, Vol. I, p. 215.

in themselves (and by a "minor" amendment I mean anything less than a change to a parliamentary system), we find that they fall into three main classes: (1) those that would improve the working of the presidential system as such (and by making its evils less obvious might help to perpetuate that system); (2) those improvements that are irrelevant to the differences between the presidential and cabinet systems; and (3) those improvements that move in the direction of cabinet government.

One change, frequently advocated, that would improve the working of the presidential system as such is the abolition of the Electoral College. The framers of the Constitution put forward the College as a device for indirect election: the people were to choose their wisest men, their best judges of intellect and character; and these men were to assemble and to choose that citizen who was most fit to be President. But being themselves chosen to make but a single decision, they were naturally called upon to tell the people in advance what their decision would be: hence they were not chosen for themselves but for their choice; they were not chosen because of their abstract qualities of judgment but because of their specific promise. The Electoral College, by a perfectly natural evolution, has therefore become a needless intermediary for registering the popular choice; it is a fifth wheel, a useless appendage.

It is, moreover, a confirmation of Bagehot's maxim that "whatever is unnecessary in government is pernicious." [1] For it has resulted in an artificial counting of the popular will, which can turn a narrow popular victory into an Electoral College "landslide," and which not only disfranchises the minority in each State *but actually makes that minority's vote count against it.* This has all sorts of unhealthy effects. On occasion it has actually reversed the popular verdict. It has meant, in practice, that no Democratic candidate for the Presidency ever campaigns in Maine or Vermont, or any Republican candidate in the "solid South." Worse, regardless of the relative inherent merits of different men, only men from "doubtful" States can be nominated for the Presidency. This effect, and not any miraculous fertility of genius in that State, explains the large number of Presidents who have come from Ohio. The result of this has been not only to restrict the range of choice of men of ability for the Presidential office but to intensify and perpetuate sectional differences. Yet an amendment to abolish the Electoral College and elect the President by direct popular vote would help to confirm and entrench the basically unsound presidential system.

2

Another amendment that would improve the working of the presidential system as such is one that was long regarded as a part of our "unwritten Constitution," but which ceased to be so on Nov. 5, 1940, when Franklin D. Roosevelt was elected for a third

[1] *The English Constitution,* p. 95.

MINOR REFORMS

term. This is an amendment to limit the President to not more than two four-year terms.

A third term, above all a third *consecutive* term for a President, is not a danger to our democratic institutions merely because there was an unbroken tradition against it until 1940. It is not a danger merely because Jefferson, Jackson, Cleveland and other great leaders in our history explicitly opposed it. The causation, in fact, is the other way around: great political leaders throughout our history as a nation opposed the third term, the tradition against it came into being and was preserved inviolate for more than a century and a half, because our leaders recognized the great danger to our democratic institutions once the two-term limit were destroyed.

The chief reason against destroying that limit is this—that a President in office running for reelection has always possessed a great and now possesses an almost overwhelming advantage over his opponent. He is not certain to win, but he starts with the scales heavily weighted in his favor.

A President begins with the huge prestige of his office behind him. This is a great psychological advantage that is seldom estimated at its real strength. His opponent must discuss him gingerly, because such divinity doth hedge his office. He and his followers need be under no such constraint, on the other hand, in discussing his opponent. A President, moreover, can "act" while his opponent can only "talk." He can conduct an effective political campaign while appearing to be concerned solely with the responsibilities of his office.

More important than these psychological factors, a President has immense powers to keep himself in office. There is, first, his power to ensure his own renomination. Unless, in the first place, an incumbent President withdraws unequivocally, the nominating convention of his party cannot name someone else without offering him a direct affront. But there is a much more powerful force at work in a nominating convention than mere embarrassment. The convention of the party in power is an army of Federal officeholders. It consists of men who either owe their own appointment to the President, or will owe their reappointment to the President, or owe to the President at the very least their power to recommend others for appointment. In short, the President in office is the candidate with whom it is most profitable to curry favor and whom it is most dangerous to oppose.

The same powers that make it possible for a President to renominate himself also go a long way toward helping him win the election. Chief among them, it has been recognized throughout our history, has been the power of patronage. As Senator Norris remarked during the Coolidge Administration:

> When this influence [patronage] is combined and used for the perpetuation in office of the head of our government, it is a danger to free institutions and strikes at the very root of democracy. Such a danger leads di-

rectly toward a monarchy and takes away from the people themselves the right to select their own chief magistrate. . . . It exists now to a greater extent than it did, because Federal offices have been multiplied many fold and partisan political machines . . . are now enthroned in power greater than ever in our history.

These arguments are becoming constantly stronger, not weaker. The army of even peacetime Federal officeholders has more than doubled since Senator Norris spoke. In addition to these direct officeholders, we have such institutions now as the WPA, and we have many other classes of recipients of Government loans, subsidies and bonuses. According to estimates made during the last campaign, there were then more than 8,000,000 persons who, although not officeholders, received aid from Federal sources. It is true that all these people were nominally free to vote for either candidate. Many of them in the last election did, in fact, vote for Mr. Willkie. But they were inevitably under pressure to vote for the President in power, because it seemed ungrateful or personally dangerous to vote against the Administration that had given them their jobs or their subsidies.

Let us add to this the enormous powers of publicity that, compared with any possible opposition, an Administration now commands. Let us add the innumerable press agents and "public-relations" men, by whatever title, who are connected with the innumerable Government agencies. All these men send out at public expense an endless stream of publicity designed to show what their agencies—and the Administration at the top—are doing for the public weal. They stand constantly ready to answer any "misrepresentation"—which often turns out in practice to mean any criticism whatever—of their agencies. Add the Cabinet members, the heads of agencies, all appointed by the President, whose salaries are paid by the taxpayer but who stand always ready to make partisan speeches supporting the Administration. Add the State machines, the powerful city machines tied to the Administration in power as never before by the hold that the distribution of unprecedentedly huge Federal relief and public-works funds gives to the Federal Government over local governments.

Add all this, and one begins to form an idea of the enormous power that a Federal Administration has today to perpetuate itself. It is true that all this cannot protect it from defeat if the President in power becomes sufficiently unpopular with the independent part of the population. But in any election that would otherwise be at all close, the Administration machine can weight the scales decisively.

It may be objected that this weighting of the scales in favor of the Administration in office would apply to a second as well as to a third consecutive term. This is true; though it is true, also, that a President in power can for various reasons become more deeply entrenched the longer he remains in power. But Thomas Jefferson gave the real reason for distinguishing between a second and a third consecutive term:

My opinion originally was that the President of the United States should have been elected for seven years and [be] forever ineligible afterward. I have since become sensible that seven years is too long to be irremovable, and that there should be a peaceable way of withdrawing a man in midway who is doing wrong. The service for eight years, with a power to remove at the end of the first four, comes nearly to my principle as corrected by experience.

One possible alternative solution to this problem would be for the Constitution, instead of limiting the number of terms, to require that a presidential candidate for office to succeed himself must resign his office not less than sixty days before the day of election. Such an alternative would meet the arguments of those who contend that a particular President has become "indispensable." A forced resignation of this sort (while the Vice President or a successor selected by Congress took over the Presidential office in the few months' interim) would do a good deal to bring the President's opponent more nearly to an equal footing with him in soliciting the voters' favor. The President seeking a new term, in such a case, would still enjoy some advantages, but they would be considerably reduced.

European commentators have long thought that Americans attach too much importance to the two-term tradition for Presidents, but that is because these commentators are themselves too accustomed to think in terms of the conditions that surround a prime minister. It matters little if the latter remains in power more than eight years or some longer term, because he is subject to removal *at any time*. But a President, elected for a third or later time, is beyond the reach of the people for another four years. A restriction on the length or number of the President's terms, in short, is an amendment that is necessary only because we have a presidential system.

Another amendment that would improve the working of the presidential system as such would be one permitting the President to veto individual items in appropriation bills. The Governors of three-quarters of the States already have this power, and it has worked well. But the principle of executive veto itself is necessary only in a presidential system, in which the executive and legislative branches are separated, and not in a parliamentary system, in which the two branches are fused, and in which one must either give way or both must immediately submit to a verdict of the people if they do not agree.

3

Among the second class of amendments—those that are irrelevant to the differences between the presidential and parliamentary systems—the most important and desirable would be one removing the existing residential requirement for Congressmen. Under the Constitution, every Representative and every Senator must when elected be an inhabitant of the State from which he is elected. On the basis of this, local laws and national custom have gone even further, so that in practice a representative must be a resident not only of the State but of the very Congressional district that elects him.

As Bryce pointed out in his generation, this restriction is harmful both to candidates, whose field of choice in seeking a constituency it narrows, and to constituencies, whom it debars from choosing persons, however eminent, who do not reside in their midst: "Inferior men are returned, because there are many parts of the country which do not grow statesmen, where nobody, or at any rate nobody desiring to enter Congress, is to be found above a moderate level of political capacity. And men of marked ability and zeal are prevented from forcing their way in." The restriction also reduces the independence of Congressmen: "A promising politician may lose his seat in his own district through some fluctuation of opinion, or perhaps because he has offended the local wire pullers by too much independence. Since he cannot find a seat elsewhere he is stranded; his political life is closed, while other young men inclined to independence take warning from his fate."

Against these serious evils, Bryce was unable to find any compensating advantages: "In Europe it is not found that a member is less active or successful in urging the local interests of his constituency because he does not live there. He is often more successful, because more personally influential or persuasive than any resident whom the constituency could supply." In England, Bryce pointed out, many ministers are necessarily members of the House of

Commons, and "the inconvenience of excluding a man from the service of the nation because he could not secure his return in the place of his residence would be unendurable. Of the last five Prime Ministers who have sat in the House of Commons," he was even able to add at the time he wrote, "none has represented his place of residence." [1]

Twenty years ago, H. L. Mencken, contributing the essay on "Politics" to a symposium on what was wrong with America, centered his attack precisely on the two sentences of the Constitution that provide, respectively, that no Representative and no Senator can be elected who is not "an inhabitant of that State in which he shall be chosen":

> I have a notion that there are few provisions of the Constitution that have had a more profound effect upon the character of practical politics in the Republic, or, indirectly, upon the general color of American thinking in the political department. They have made steadily for parochialism in legislation, for the security and prosperity of petty local bosses and machines, for the multiplication of pocket and rotten boroughs of the worst sort, and, above all, for the progressive degeneration of the honesty and honor of representatives. They have greased the ways for the trashy and ignoble fellow who aspires to get into Congress, and they have blocked them for the man of sense, dignity, and self-respect. More, perhaps, than any other single influence they have been responsible for the present debauched and degraded condition of the two houses, and particularly of the lower

[1] *The American Commonwealth*, Vol. I, pp. 191-195.

MINOR REFORMS

one. Find me the worst ass in Congress, and I'll show you a man they have helped to get there and to stay there. Find me the most shameless scoundrel, and I'll show you another.[1]

In the hope that it may clinch the argument for reform in this case, if only by varied repetition, I offer one more quotation, this time from Harold J. Laski:

No constituency ought to be limited in choice, as in the United States, to one of its own residents. Nothing is so certain to make for parochialism. Nothing more tempts a member to lend himself to the service of sinister interests than knowledge that defeat may mean the end of his political career. It is, moreover, a serious waste on another side. The ability at the command of a State does not distribute itself with mathematical accuracy over the electoral divisions. New York is more likely to have a number of men capable of playing a distinguished part in the Senate than Delaware or Nevada. A theory which equates defeat with practically permanent exile does not maximise the advantages of a community. It is all to the good that Mr. Gladstone, defeated in Oxford, should find refuge in South Lancashire, and Mr. Churchill move from Manchester to Dundee. Any other view under-estimates so seriously the importance of experienced leadership in politics as to make it not unlikely that it is at bottom built upon the credulous superstition that, all men being more or less equal in ability, the composition of a legislature is not a very serious matter. This is a mistake so profound that not the least cause, for

[1] *Civilization in the United States.* An Inquiry by Thirty Americans, edited by Harold E. Stearns (1922).

example, of the declining respect for the Congress of the United States is its failure to contain the natural leaders of the people.[1]

Americans deplore frequently enough our shameless waste of political skill and training; our failure, as compared with the English, to keep in active public service the men who have finally come to know something about the very difficult art of government. Thomas E. Dewey, writing in the *Reader's Digest* of February, 1941, pointed out that:

There are eight men in this country today who have had unusual opportunity to study the science of government, who have learned at first hand the needs and demands of the people and were called upon to voice those needs and demands, and who have received the popular support of more citizens on Election Day than any official in the nation except the President. Yet today these men—four Republicans and four Democrats—are in private life.

The men he referred to were former President Herbert Hoover, Wendell L. Willkie, Alfred M. Landon, Alfred E. Smith, John W. Davis, James M. Cox, John Nance Garner, and Charles G. Dawes. Wrote Mr. Dewey:

For 150 years men have discussed the necessity of bringing into the government the ablest men in the country. Yet we have ignored the most obvious means to that end. The time has come to stop this waste of brilliant leadership by amending the Constitution so that

[1] *A Grammar of Politics* (1925), pp. 318-319.

every ex-President, every ex-Vice President, and every presidential nominee receiving the second largest number of votes may become, for life, United States Senator-at-Large.

There can be no doubt regarding the desirability of the end that Mr. Dewey has in mind, but serious questions may be raised concerning the means he proposes to achieve it. The principle of life tenure for policy-making legislators, particularly when some of these are men who have been rejected by the voters at the polls, would run counter to American democratic traditions. Mr. Dewey suggests—for convincing reasons—that these men should probably not be granted a vote in the Senate. But the deprivation of the power to vote would itself be a source of embarrassment. Inability to influence the decision of the Senate in any direct way would undermine the influence and prestige of these men, and give them both an inward sense and an outward air of futility.

If the plan Mr. Dewey suggests were in fact the only means of securing the essential object that he has in view, its benefits might well be held to outweigh its defects. But its essential object could be much better achieved, it seems to me, by a constitutional amendment removing the foolish residential qualification for members of either House of Congress. If this were done, their respective political parties could run these men from "safe" constituencies. Thinly populated States or small-town constituencies would vie with each other for the honor and publicity of nominating and electing them. In addition, through this method, a score or more of very able former Senators or Representatives, now consigned to private life because they were defeated in their home States or districts, could return to Congress. Moreover, men of national eminence would be glad to run for a seat even in the House of Representatives if that body reformed its own internal organization to permit such men to function properly. John Quincy Adams, after he had been President, did not consider it beneath his dignity to run for election and to serve as a member of the House of Representatives for seventeen years until his death.

If American candidates, in brief, could run for election in any State or district, regardless of the place of their own residence, it would enormously improve the average caliber of our Representatives or Senators at the same time that it would strengthen party discipline and help our national parties to stand for real differences in issues and policies. In a State or district in which a Senator or Representative calling himself a Democrat or Republican in fact disregarded the principal policies for which his declared party stood, the national party leaders would not have to depend on the candidates locally available, but could oppose any candidate falsely making use of the party label with one of their strongest and best known candidates. They could also reward an able man, unable to secure office from his home district, by running him elsewhere. This form of party discipline would involve the least harm with the greatest benefits, for it would never be successful unless the particular voters who were appealed to approved it.

4

Another amendment that would be largely irrelevant to the essential differences between the cabinet and presidential form of government would be one reforming the Supreme Court. The ostensible purpose of Franklin Roosevelt's proposed court reform—to bring "younger blood" into the court—was altogether desirable; but the method he proposed was altogether obnoxious. A proper constitutional amendment would make retirement from the court on a pension either compulsory at the age of seventy, or perhaps voluntary at seventy and compulsory at seventy-five. But no amendment should permit the Supreme Court to be "packed" by an increase in its membership adopted to change its line of decisions. On the contrary, the present very dangerous loophole in the Constitution in this respect should be tightly closed. The membership of the Supreme Court should be fixed by constitutional amendment definitely at the present number of nine.

The wisdom and necessity of such a protection was made plain by President Roosevelt's 1937 proposal, and was recognized more than a generation before in a prophetic passage in Bryce:

> The Fathers of the Constitution studied nothing more than to secure the complete independence of the judiciary. The President was not permitted to remove the

judges, nor Congress to diminish their salaries. One thing only was either forgotten or deemed undesirable, because highly inconvenient, to determine—the number of judges in the Supreme Court. Here was a weak point, a joint in the court's armor through which a weapon might some day penetrate. . . . As the Constitution does not prescribe the number of justices, a statute may increase or diminish the number as Congress thinks fit. . . . This method is plainly susceptible of . . . dangerous application. Suppose a Congress and President bent on doing something which the Supreme Court deems contrary to the Constitution. They pass a statute. A case arises under it. The court on the hearing of the case unanimously declares the statute to be null, as being beyond the powers of Congress. Congress forthwith passes and the President signs another statute more than doubling the number of justices. The President appoints to the new justiceships men who are pledged to hold the former statute constitutional. The Senate confirms his appointments. Another case raising the validity of the disputed statute is brought up to the court. The new justices outvote the old ones: the statute is held valid: the security provided for the protection of the Constitution is gone like a morning mist.[1]

Protection would be secured from such a danger by the simple expedient of fixing the membership of the Supreme Court by constitutional amendment definitely at nine.

It is important that the legislative and executive branches of the government be fused, as they are in

[1] *The American Commonwealth*, Vol. I, pp. 276-277.

England, but this does not mean that the judicial should be fused with them. Here is where the doctrine of the separation of powers has its legitimate application. It is an historic function of the courts to protect against executive caprice, injustice or discrimination. Under a federal government and a written constitution, the legislature cannot be permitted to be its own judge of the scope of its powers. The courts must protect citizens against either legislative or executive usurpation. They can do this only if their own independence of the legislature or executive is protected. For this purpose the constitutional provision for life terms (or terms until a fixed age, with pension protection) is admirably adapted, as would also be provision for a fixed number of Supreme Court justices.

Nevertheless, more flexibility would be desirable in the removal of judges than at present exists. The Constitution (Art. III, Sec. 1) provides that the judges of both the Supreme and inferior courts "shall hold their offices during good behavior." This has been taken in practice to mean that they can be removed only on impeachment proceedings, and these, in turn, have been by implication restricted in their application only to "treason, bribery, or other high crimes and misdemeanors"—the conditions set down in Art. II, Sec. 4, of the Constitution as necessary for the removal of "the President, Vice President and all civil officers of the United States."

But there are obviously other conditions under

which it is desirable to remove judges. One would be the case of mental derangement (even if the deterioration caused by excessive age is assumed to be already provided for by a definite constitutional age limit). More important in the probable need for its application would be the possibility of removing a judge who was habitually usurping congressional legislative functions—a depressingly frequent habit. No doubt a judge, conscientiously trying to interpret a vague law in a particular case, sometimes unavoidably "makes" law in trying to guess the intent of the framers or to apply some "rule of reason." But if a judge gives strained interpretations, particularly if these are in consonance with some openly boasted "social philosophy" of his own that may not be shared by Congress, Congress should be able to remove him. Otherwise there is danger that the Supreme Court could become a third legislative body more powerful than Congress and beyond its reach, or beyond the reach of the people.

This problem could be met, I suggest, by granting Congress a constitutional power to remove Federal judges without impeachment proceedings, provided, say, that not more than one such judge could be so removed in any one year. Such removal could be either by a majority of both Houses with the concurrence of the President, or by two-thirds of each House. This would provide a method, though one of rare use, for dealing with extremely capricious or incompetent judges, or judges who dangerously usurp the legislative function. It would be a far more limited power of removal than that now enjoyed by the British Parliament. It would safeguard judicial independence but provide at least some curb against judicial usurpation.

XI

IN THE RIGHT DIRECTION

IN THE last chapter we considered a few of the constitutional reforms that would strengthen presidential government by removing more obvious evils, and a few of the reforms irrelevant to the difference between presidential and cabinet government. We come now to that third class of constitutional amendments which would at least move in the general direction of responsible cabinet government.

Among these are amendments that would reduce the prerogatives and powers of the Senate. No parliamentary government can be made to work where there are two houses of equal and coordinate powers. For one house can nullify the policy of the other; and there is no way to ensure agreement between them, and to establish a government that can act with vigor and sureness in a crisis, unless one house must ultimately give way to the other.

Under our Constitution, the power to ratify treaties not only belongs to the Senate alone, but requires a vote of two-thirds of the Senate. Obviously, to permit the ratification of treaties by a majority vote of both the House and Senate would be a much more satisfactory arrangement. It is, in the first place, pointlessly illogical that it should require a majority of the House and a mere majority of the Senate to make war, but that it should require two-thirds of the Senate to make peace. The same majorities that are authorized to do the first should be authorized to do the second.

The requirement for ratification of treaties by a two-thirds vote places the power of indefinitely prolonged obstruction in the hands of a minority. It was largely responsible for America's refusal to enter the League of Nations or to adhere to the World Court. "The irreparable mistake of our Constitution," wrote John Hay in a letter in 1899, when he was Secretary of State, "puts it into the power of one-third + 1 of the Senate to meet with a categorical veto any treaty negotiated by the President, even though it may have the approval of nine-tenths of the people of the nation." As Harold Laski has remarked: "The knowledge that a little bloc of recalcitrant senators may hold up or modify a wise proposal has adverse effect both upon the prospect of embarking upon it and upon the process of negotiation itself."

Here is an amendment of the greatest urgency if the President is not to be hamstrung in negotiating treaties, after the present war, in which America will at last assume its responsibilities in helping to bring and to guarantee a sound and durable world peace.

This amendment alone, however, would bring only part of the change that is really necessary. Ray Stannard Baker, in his volume on Woodrow Wilson, wrote:

It has been made impossible for America to speak with a bold and united voice. Nearly every important treaty the country has been called upon to make has become a bone of contention between the executive and the Senate. It is certain that in the years to come, if we are to go forward in the new paths and stand for a clear-cut world policy, we must devise some method of speaking to the world promptly and with an undivided voice. Our present system leads to utter weakness, muddle, and delay: it forces both sides to play politics, and instead of meeting the issue squarely to indulge in a vast controversy over the prerogatives of two co-ordinate branches of the government. The deadlock between the Executive and the Senate every time we face a really critical foreign problem is intolerable. It not only disgraces us before the nations, but in some future world crisis may ruin us.[1]

To take away the power from "one-third plus one" of the Senate to block a treaty, and to provide for ratification by a simple majority of the Senate and House, would mitigate the evil of which Mr. Baker complains, but would not cure it. Only the adoption of a full parliamentary system would cure it.

2

I have spoken earlier of an amendment to permit the President to veto particular items in appropriation bills. Quite as useful—with the advantage that it would move in the direction of parliamentary government—would be an amendment that would permit

[1] *Woodrow Wilson and the World Settlement* (1922), Vol. I, p. 316.

the Senate, as now, to reduce the appropriations of the House for any purpose, *but forbid it to raise them.* This restriction on the power of the upper house exists in several constitutions abroad. It would seem to accord with the real intentions of many of the framers of the Constitution. They provided that "all bills for raising revenue" must *originate* in the House of Representatives. But by allowing the Senate to propose amendments, they turned this into a merely technical provision of little practical importance. In practice the Senate can increase appropriations or taxes by as large a sum as it pleases, enjoying as many rights as the House in this respect. The Senate, unfortunately, has shown itself far more irresponsible in making appropriations even than the House: it is continually writing up appropriations, and getting its way in conference.

A statement by the Citizens Emergency Committee on Nondefense Expenditures on June 6, 1942, for example, pointed out that in every case in six recent departmental-appropriation bills the Senate had increased the amount:

Title	As passed House	As passed Senate
Independent offices	$2,096,048,875	$2,126,042,891
Treasury and post office	1,112,926,899	1,113,321,439
Agriculture	648,170,517	680,395,695
State, commerce and justice	221,078,100	425,703,235
Interior	162,157,965	186,924,998
Legislative	27,463,866	27,884,588
	$4,267,846,223	$4,560,272,846

This record is typical, not exceptional. It is the result of an entirely natural process: individual Senators cannot strengthen their political position merely by endorsing the appropriations already made by the House: they must show some vicarious generosity of their own.

The ghastly state of our Federal finances after the war will make some curb on expenditures, by both the President and the Senate, imperative. If the Senate had the power to curb appropriations but not to increase them, it would use the power to curb far more than it does now. One reason why Senators do not cut House appropriations today is that the House in retaliation would cut *their* appropriations. But if Senators could not make their own added appropriations for local purposes, to increase votes in their particular States, they would have nothing to lose by cutting House appropriations. Not only would Senators cease in such a case to engage in "logrolling" for each other; they would do no logrolling for the House.

3

A "minor" amendment to the Constitution that in certain emergencies would bring the country more in accord with the practice in parliamentary countries is one abolishing the office of Vice President.

Our Vice Presidency is a peculiar institution, which few other countries, even the Latin-American republics which have followed our own Constitution so closely in other respects, have seen fit to imitate. The most important function of the American

Vice President is usually served before he assumes the office at all—that is, during the few months while he is merely a candidate. Then he "balances the ticket." At best this is a geographical balance (dictated mainly by the vicious Electoral College method of counting ballots). At worst, and much too frequently, the ticket is "balanced" by nominating for Vice President a man who believes precisely the opposite on leading issues from what the candidate for President believes. If the presidential candidate has a reputation for conservatism, a "radical" is named so that the ticket will not look too conservative; the reverse process takes place if the presidential candidate is reputed to be too "radical."

After his election the Vice President has nothing to do but preside over the Senate. A Vice President is certainly not essential for this function: there is no reason why the Senate, like the House, cannot elect its own presiding officer. By custom the Vice President keeps his mouth shut in public on all political issues. The result of this, as burlesqued in the musical-comedy figure Mr. Throttlebottom, is that many able men refuse the Vice Presidential nomination, and even imply that it is a sort of insult for them to be mentioned in connection with it.

The chief reason why the Vice Presidency is esteemed at all is that it carries with it a fair statistical chance of becoming President. Nine of the thirty-three Vice Presidents, more than one in four, have gone on to be President. Those who did so through the death of the preceding President were Tyler, Fillmore, Johnson, Arthur, Theodore Roosevelt and Coolidge.

Considering the party motives and general conditions that surround the nomination for Vice President, the country has been luckier on the average in the caliber of the Vice Presidents who became President than might have been expected. But this relative good luck may not continue.

If the aim of a constitution is either to clarify the expression of the popular will or to bring the ablest men of a country into leadership, the institution of the Vice Presidency achieves neither purpose. On the contrary, the institution beclouds campaign issues. It forces many voters to choose a man they do not like in order to elect a man they do like. It would be an obvious improvement in our democratic machinery if only candidates for President were nominated and elected, and if the Constitution were amended to provide, following the precedent in a number of other countries, that in the event of the death of the President the successor to fill his unexpired term would be chosen by the House and Senate sitting as a single body. A President so chosen would be certain to be an outstanding man, who would receive the willing cooperation of Congress, and would represent the sentiment of the country at the time he came into office.

Such a man could not fail to be a better choice, on the average, than a man who comes to the Presidency accidentally through the death of the President. Congress, in making its own choice of a successor, would be forced to act with the utmost seriousness and responsibility. Compare this with the irresponsible and frivolous attitude of a party nominating convention that chooses a Vice-Presidential candidate with little real belief that he will ever become President—and with even a real doubt whether he will ever become Vice President! The superiority of the method of Congressional choice is beyond question.

If we carry the logic of this method somewhat further, and say that Congress should also be able to change the executive if it finds that it has made a mistake, but that the incumbent executive should have the reciprocal right to appeal to the verdict of the people against that of Congress, we have arrived at the fundamentals of the parliamentary system!

4

The present chapter is written on the probability that, however urgent it may be for the United States to adopt a full parliamentary form of government, the American people may not be quickly brought to recognize the need for such a change, and that therefore those who favor it may have to decide what sound compromises they will meanwhile support if these seem to have a better chance of adoption. This assumption is no doubt at least partially defeatist, but it is a necessary one for realists to make. If those who favor constitutional reform were to look at the weight of the arguments for it in the past seventy-five years and at the cogency with which the case for constitutional reform has been put by a handful of writers, and contrast this with sluggishness of the great body of opinion, and the failure to make even the most obviously desirable reforms, they might well have reason for despair. One reason, however, for lack of past success is that the advocates of constitutional revision have thought it sufficient merely to state, as forcibly as they personally could, the need for such revision. They have neglected to consider what persons less disinterested than themselves do not neglect —*a technique for converting public opinion.*

I am not about to launch upon an essay on the principles of advertising or publicity, or to repeat those Machiavellian maxims on the nature of effective propaganda to be found in Adolf Hitler's *Mein Kampf*. I should like here to put forward only two suggestions.

The first of these is that agitation for constitutional reform need not confine itself in America to reform of the Federal Government. If properly directed it may make substantial inroads in the case of the States and municipalities. The States have been an amazingly neglected field in this respect. The historic relation of the Federal Constitution to those of the States is an instructive one. The Federal Constitution is based to a much larger extent than is generally recognized on the various state constitutions existing before the Federal Convention of 1787. But since the Federal Constitution has been in existence, all the new States admitted to the union have imitated it almost slavishly.

Though there are forty-eight different state constitutions, though they have been frequently amended, and though many of them have been fully revised by conventions, not once but several times, the lack of enterprise, imagination or courage in these revisions has been extraordinary. Each has an executive, the Governor, separated from the legislature, and serving for a rigidly fixed term, usually with veto and similar powers closely modeled on those of the Presidency. Each legislature consists of two houses of virtually equal powers. (The only present exception is the one-house legislature of Nebraska, adopted largely through the influence of Senator George W. Norris.)[1]

Though the legislature is frequently of a different political complexion from the Governor, though the majority of one house in the legislature is frequently Republican and the other Democratic, and though this situation brings about chronic deadlocks, squabbles, jockeying for position, demagogy and bitter recriminations, instead of a quiet and constructive attention to the real business of the State, the situation seems to be blandly tolerated year after year. One would almost think that Americans considered it the real function of politicians to "put on a good show," regardless of the effect on the public welfare, rather than to govern efficiently and wisely. And, in fact, the kind of interest that many Americans do take in politics is more akin to the interest in a horse race or a prize fight than to the interest in government as a

[1] See JOHN P. SENNING, *The One-House Legislature* (1937).

difficult problem, a business, a profession or an art.

But the real reason for the complacency with which Americans seem to regard chronic political deadlocks is, I am convinced, lack of understanding of their underlying cause. When there is a deadlock, the Governor blames the legislature and the legislature blames the Governor, or the lower House blames the upper and the upper House blames the lower. The public almost inevitably looks at the issue in the terms in which the politicians state it. It tries hopelessly to find out which of the three agencies is *really* to blame for a particular deadlock. It thereby fails to recognize that the state constitution itself, by setting up three separate and independent agencies, each capable of blocking or vetoing the decision of the other, has made a constant series of deadlocks inevitable. The remedy lies in revising the Constitution, in concentrating the power of ultimate decision in a *single* agency, and *holding that agency responsible for its proper use*. This means the adoption of cabinet government.

But to make clear to the public the necessity for this, there must be individuals or private organizations that will make it their business, every time such a deadlock arises, to pass over the merits of the particular point at issue, which will receive discussion enough in any event, and to point to the *constitutional* set-up that has made the deadlock possible, if not, indeed, unavoidable.

5

Before discussing the technique by which this may be done, I should like to say a word about the municipalities. Here, at last, is the one point in American government where political enterprise and adventurousness have been manifest, the one point where real inventiveness has been shown, the one point where parliamentary or cabinet government (though it masquerades under another name) has been tried.

It is instructive to recall that it was first tried only after a disaster, and then almost by accident rather than design. In September, 1900, a tidal wave swept in from the gulf and wiped out part of the city of Galveston, Tex. Until that time the city had been governed by the usual set-up of mayor, board of aldermen, and various other elected officials, each with independent powers. The flood created a grave emergency. The city was faced by bankruptcy. The state legislature was asked to intervene. It abolished the old city government and vested all powers in the hands of five commissioners. By majority vote these commissioners (who after 1903 were made elective) could enact the city ordinances, appropriate money, levy taxes, borrow on the credit of the city and make all appointments. The administrative work of the city was to be divided into four departments, which four of the commissioners were to apportion among themselves. The fifth commissioner, the mayor president, was to exercise a coordinating supervision. The plan was looked upon as an emergency measure, a sort of municipal receivership. It was expected that when normal conditions were restored the old type of government would be established again. The results, however, convinced the people of Galveston that the plan ought to be continued permanently. The "commission plan" began to attract widespread attention throughout the country, and other cities adopted it.[1]

The commission plan, however, though it is still used in some cities, has proved more successful as a protest than as a form of government. As William B. Munro has put it: "The commission as a legislative body is too small to be adequately representative, while as an executive authority it is too cumbrous to be efficient. It is a five-headed executive, a pyramid without a peak."

But the commission plan has served as the inspiration for a radically important forward step in city government. The credit for this improvement seems to be principally due to Richard S. Childs. Commission government, according to its advocates, was "just like a corporation with its board of directors." Mr. Childs saw that this "catch phrase has converted whole cities," but remarked that the commission would not be like a board of directors until it would "appoint a manager who in turn would hire the departmental heads, reporting regularly to the commission and submitting to it only broad matters of policy."[2]

[1] Cf. "Commission System of Government," *Encyclopaedia of the Social Sciences*.
[2] See Don K. Price, "The Promotion of the City Manager Plan," *The Public Opinion Quarterly* (Winter, 1941).

Out of this grew the city-manager, or, more accurately, the council-manager, plan. This plan consists in essence of the election of a small council, which thereupon selects one of its members to serve as mayor ("chairman of the board") and then appoints some expert administrator, often from some other city, as "city manager" to do the real administrative work and appoint the other city officials.

The position of city manager was first created in 1909 by the council of Staunton, Va., a city then under the mayor and council form of government. In 1912, Sumter, S. C., was the first city to adopt the full commission-manager form of government. When the plan was adopted by Dayton, Ohio, in 1914, it came into national prominence. Today it exists in nearly 500 cities.

Now it is instructive to notice that the city-manager form of government, though in essence similar to the parliamentary form, was not suggested by the parliamentary form and not adopted in any conscious emulation of it. On the contrary, it was adopted in conscious emulation of the way in which a great business firm is organized. The chief differences between the council-manager and parliamentary form of government are two: in the orthodox parliamentary form, the chief executive is chosen from among the members of the legislative body itself; in the council-manager form, he is drawn from outside. In the parliamentary form, the executive so chosen has the right to dissolve the body that chose him and appeal to the people for a verdict; in the council-manager plan, the manager may be removed by a majority of the council and cannot appeal to the people (though this was unfortunately also the position of the Premier under the Third French Republic). But the council-manager plan shares with parliamentary government two great virtues: the fusion of legislative and executive power, and the flexibility that permits at least the executive to be removed when he has shown himself either unwilling or unable to carry out the legislative will.

Another and more important parallel is suggested by this one. As between the two, it is the parliamentary form of government that is the more natural and spontaneous, and the presidential form that is labored and contrived. The parliamentary form is the almost inevitable form that thousands of corporations, with great freedom of choice in fixing their own organization, have adopted.

In practice, it should be added, the council-manager plan is often found with both merits and defects that are the result of traditions not essential to it. One of its good traditions has been the habit of going *outside the city*, when necessary, to choose an expert city manager, a tradition particularly valuable for small cities, which are thus not made dependent upon the accidents of local training and talent. One of the bad traditions of the council-manager plan has been the association built up by some reformers between it and proportional representation. Advocates of P.R. would give the impression, indeed, that P.R. is the real and main reform achieved by the council-manager plan. Not only, however, is P.R. not essential to the plan; it is harmful to it and contrary to its spirit, which requires a coherent majority for unified and prompt decisions.

6

I remarked a while back that I should like to put forward two suggestions regarding a technique for converting American public opinion to the parliamentary form of government. The first of these was that the agitation for constitutional reform need not confine itself in America to the Federal Government, but might find a fruitful field in the States and particularly in the municipalities. Such reform in municipal and state governments, it should be pointed out, would be important not only for its own sake, and to the particular cities and States concerned, but for its effect on reform of the Federal Constitution. If only one State had the intelligence, imagination and courage to adopt a parliamentary form of government, the good effect on the prospects for Federal constitutional reform would be incalculable. Americans are traditionally—some of them are even pathologically—suspicious of "foreign" ideas in the political and economic realm. (In the realm of science and invention, however, common sense forces them to recognize that the national origin of an idea is irrelevant to its truth or value.) The example of a parliamentary government at home, even on a small scale, would therefore be of immense value in breaking down this prejudice.

The second suggestion that I wish to make with regard to a technique for converting American public opinion to parliamentary government is the organization of a *League for Constitutional Reform*. The occasional, spasmodic, unorganized advocacy of individuals will be ineffective. Experience has shown that organized bodies are necessary to affect the great sluggish mass of public opinion. If these bodies are organized for ill-advised purposes, like the old Anti-Saloon League, or to pursue the selfish interests of a small group, like various labor, farm, war-veteran, high-tariff and public-utility organizations, they are capable of doing great harm. But many of them have done immense good. Private organizations such as the Citizens Union and Citizens Budget Commission in New York City, or like the National Municipal League, the National Economy League or the Foreign Policy Association in the Federal field, to name only a handful out of many, have had an incalculable effect in informing, influencing and educating American public opinion.

A League for Constitutional Reform, as I see it, would confine itself to discussing the constitutional aspects of public questions. It would advocate a parliamentary form of government for cities, States, and for the nation. It would be organized on a national scale and have state and city chapters. The city chapters would support the council-manager plan for their own cities and would petition state legislatures to empower cities to adopt the plan. When a mayor fell out with his board of aldermen, or a governor with his legislature, or one legislative house with another, or the President with Congress, the League would not attempt to fix the various degrees of individual blame or responsibility. Its comments on the particular situations, as they arose, would be confined to showing that it was not the individual stubbornness or wickedness of the governor or the legislature that was causing the deadlock, but that the primary fault lay in the mistaken system of "checks and balances" which made possible and encouraged these chronic antagonisms. By patiently and relentlessly calling attention to this underlying constitutional factor, the League could not fail in time to make the American public recognize the basic constitutional cause of the quarrels, deadlocks, paralysis and shifting of responsibility (more popularly known as "buck passing") so characteristic of American political life. Once this basic constitutional cause was recognized clearly and widely enough, reform would be almost certain to follow.

"But can we wait for all this?" the reader may ask. It is a grave question. Federal constitutional reform has become imperative, particularly if the nation is to organize itself with that remorseless efficiency necessary to conduct a successful war against the most powerful military alliance that the world has ever known. Will we fail to reform our democracy in time to choose the leadership that we really want, give it full powers of action and hold it strictly accountable for the use of those powers? Will our reform be negligible and tardy? Will it be one more case, in the democracies, of Too Little and Too Late? Only the American people can provide the answer.

XII

TO REFORM CONGRESS FROM WITHIN

THERE is one great improvement in our government that I have reserved for a special chapter, not only because it is inherently so important but because we could make it, if we would, without changing the Constitution at all. This is a change in the *internal organization* of Congress.

It is not generally recognized—least of all, it appears, is it recognized within that body itself—that the inefficiency, aimlessness and irresponsibility of Congress are mainly the result of its own internal organization. This internal organization has always puzzled and astonished discerning native and foreign observers. There have been some important internal changes in Congress since the young Woodrow Wilson wrote his *Congressional Government* in 1884; yet the main criticisms that he made nearly sixty years ago still apply today. Our government, he pointed out, was "a government by the *standing committees* of Congress":

The leaders of the House are the chairmen of the principal standing committees. Indeed, to be exactly accurate, the House has as many leaders as there are subjects of legislation; for there are as many standing committees as there are leading classes of legislation. . . . The chairmen of the standing committees do not constitute a cooperative body like a ministry. They do not consult and concur in the adoption of homogeneous and mutually helpful measures; there is no thought of acting in concert. Each committee goes its own way at its own pace. It is impossible to discover any unity or method in the disconnected and therefore unsystematic, confused, and desultory action of the House, or any common purpose in the measures which its committees from time to time recommend.[1]

Wilson accurately described this form of organization of the House as "an odd device of *disintegration*. The House virtually both deliberates and legislates in small sections." [2] One result of the system, as he also saw, was to "shift the theatre of debate upon legislation from the floor of Congress to the privacy of the committee-rooms." [3] And he recognized further that the private and unpublished debates within the committees, however important such debates may be in themselves, are not a substitute for public debate on the floor of Congress:

The chief, and unquestionably the most essential, object of all discussion of public business is the enlightenment of public opinion; and, of course, since it cannot hear the debates of the committees, the nation is not apt to be much instructed by them. Only the committees

[1] *Congressional Government*, pp. 60-61.
[2] *Ibid.*, pp. 66-67.
[3] *Ibid.*, p. 81.

are enlightened. . . . A committee is commissioned, not to instruct the public, but to instruct and guide the House.[1]

That the most essential object of public debate on the floor of Congress is to enlighten public opinion is a fact that the House of Representatives has not been brought to recognize to this day. It has passed laws of the utmost importance, sometimes laws that have done incalculable harm, laws, in any case, that directly affect the welfare of millions of people, after the briefest possible debate. For the famous Wagner labor relations act of 1935, which might excusably have required several weeks of public discussion, the Rules Committee permitted the House just *three hours* of general debate! The Wage-Hour act of 1938, directly controlling the great mass of workers and employers, was debated and passed by the House all within a single day's session.

When they have been criticized for such shocking performances, members of the House have thought it sufficient to reply that the bill in question was under *committee* consideration for so-and-so-many days, weeks or months. They have sometimes added that debate does not change the votes in Congress anyway. What these arguments fail to recognize is that not until a bill is reported to Congress and debated on the floor do either Congressmen in general or the public at large begin to have an idea of what it is about. It requires at least a few days for public

[1] *Ibid.*, p. 83.

opinion, in and through the press, to mobilize, crystallize or express itself. It requires a little time for Congress to know what intelligent public opinion is. When general debate runs for less than a single day, none of these things can happen. If the Senate sometimes debates too much, the House always (publicly) debates important bills too little. It is one of the chief reasons why individual members and the House itself have so little prestige in the country. Yet the leaders of the House remain singularly blind to this fact.

"There are in Congress," Wilson continued, "no authoritative leaders who are the recognized spokesmen of their parties. Power is nowhere concentrated; it is rather deliberately and of set policy scattered amongst many small chiefs. . . . [Yet] the more power is divided the more irresponsible it becomes." [1] In short, "We are ruled by a score and a half of 'little legislatures.' Our legislation is conglomerate, not homogeneous. . . . Only a very small part of [Congress's] most important business can be done well; the system provides for having the rest of it done miserably, and the whole of it taken together done at haphazard." [2]

The system that Woodrow Wilson so described and condemned has not basically changed. The House today, as when he wrote, has forty-seven standing committees. The Senate has thirty-three. These "little legislatures" compete against each other for jurisdiction and power as much as ever. The heads of these

[1] *Ibid.*, pp. 92 and 93.
[2] *Ibid.*, pp. 113-114.

committees still get their posts, as in 1884, by "seniority in Congressional service," and not by ability or because they represent the views of Congress as a whole on a subject. On the contrary, to cite a single recent example, the Labor Committee of the House does not today represent the views of the House on labor legislation: the amendments to the Wagner act, passed by the last House, and the Smith bill passed by the present House (the Seventy-seventh Congress), had to come through the Judiciary Committee.

The cure for this situation I have already outlined in Chaps. VI and VII, in the discussion there of the proper internal organization of a legislative body. With present constitutional provisions, it is true, Congress cannot establish a central committee with the full powers of a cabinet. The President, standing outside Congress, would still retain his veto power, his treaty-making powers, the great power that goes with his power of appointment, the great prestige and influence of his office. But Congress nevertheless could without a change in the Constitution establish a central committee. It could appoint this committee precisely as a cabinet is appointed: Congress could name one man as leader, and give him the power of naming the other members of the central committee. The leader so chosen and his associates would probably all be members of the majority party. Congress could allow such a body to initiate its legislation, to prepare bills, to prepare a legislative program to submit to Congress and a time table for debate, and to perform the other functions that a cabinet normally performs. The result would be an enormous gain in Congressional efficiency, responsibility and prestige. Congress, at last, could have its own intelligent, coherent, legislative program. Such a central committee would be small enough, as Congress is not, to be taken into the President's confidence in wartime. It would also be powerful enough, particularly if it was of the President's own party, to demand such confidence. It could be, in short, a constant consultative body, far better equipped than Congres is at present either to effectuate presidential policies or to offer constructive criticism of them.

If such a central committee were to be effective, there would necessarily have to be turned over to it some of the chief powers today exercised by the four-score "little legislatures" within the two Houses of Congress. These specialized standing committees would not need to be abolished: on the contrary, as we saw on page 140, they could still perform very useful functions of holding hearings, of consultation, and of criticism. But their present powers of preparing and initiating legislation, and certainly their present powers of smothering legislation, would be taken from them. These would necessarily be the prerogatives of the central committee.

A possible misconception needs to be removed at this point. Such a central committee would not give, and could not give, the same kind of attention to detail that the various standing committees now do. If it made any such attempt, it would be hopelessly swamped. It would, instead, have full powers to ap-

TO REFORM CONGRESS FROM WITHIN

point expert groups and commissions to study problems, and powers to direct experts in the government departments, or special committees outside Congress, to prepare bills in accordance with its general instructions. It would do, in short, what a well-organized and conducted cabinet now does.

2

A reformed internal organization of Congress of the sort just outlined would be *legally* possible within the framework of our Constitution as it stands. But we must admit, in all candor, that it would confront serious practical and psychological obstacles. Under the Constitution, for example, the House and Senate are chambers of practically equal legislative power. It is extremely unlikely that either would submit to the leadership of a chairman of such a central committee chosen from the ranks of the other house. Moreover, it could easily happen, as it has so often in the past, that the majority in one house would be Republican and in the other Democratic. All this need not prevent, however, the creation of a small central committee by each house, each leading its own house, and meeting frequently in joint session to consult and to iron out differences. Such a divided committee would not be so satisfactory as a single committee, but it would be an immense improvement over the present Congressional organization.

I have already indicated in Chap. IV the immense practical difficulty of a reform of this sort. The present heads of the standing committees would oppose it because it would undermine their prerogatives; the minority heads or those next in line would oppose it because they would feel close to enjoying such prerogatives; those in Congress who have no great committee powers would fear to advocate it unless they were assured in advance of its success, because their present hopes for preferment depend on the favor of the existing committee heads. In addition, there stand opposed to such a change all the forces of long usage and custom.

But that such a development is not impossible is proved by the progress made in the last decade in the creation of "legislative councils" in more than a half dozen of the States. Usually composed of a small number of experienced legislators, and aided by expert advisors, these councils meet between sessions to prepare comprehensive legislative programs for submission to the legislatures. The councils are designed primarily to provide responsible and informed legislative leadership, to promote continuity in the legislative process, and to afford greater opportunity for the expert drafting of legislation. First established in Wisconsin in 1931, legislative councils were set up in Kansas and Michigan in 1933, in Virginia and Kentucky in 1936, and in Connecticut, Nebraska and Illinois in 1937.[1]

There does not seem to have been much recogni-

[1] See BRYANT PUTNEY, "Legislative Councils," *Editorial Research Reports* (1937), Washington, D. C.

tion, even among the States that have adopted the device of legislative councils, that what they were doing in effect was to take a long but incompleted step toward cabinet government as practiced in England. The legislative councils have been almost always, like the standing committees in Congress, bodies representing both parties in the legislature. Some students have conceived their function as being that of an agency for harmonizing differences between parties, between houses, and between governor and legislature. Obviously, however, they can be only of minor use in this connection. As long as state governments are built slavishly on the Federal model; as long as they make a fetish of the "separation of powers," creating bicameral legislatures with houses of equal standing, one of which is frequently dominated by one party while the second is dominated by another; as long as they have governors with veto powers who are often of a different party from that of the legislative majority, then the probability of constant deadlock and recrimination is built firmly into the state governmental structure, and the device of legislative councils, although it may act as an oil or a salve, cannot cure the basic disease. Perhaps the greatest use of the legislative councils in the end will be that of an educational device pointing toward the benefits of a full cabinet system.

Meanwhile, if Congress tries to operate in its customary manner in the present total war, it is likely to lose both prestige and power. To the extent that Congress shows itself to be inefficient or irresponsible the public will lose patience with its efforts to influence the course of events. More seriously than ever before, Congress must consider the necessity of reforming itself from within.

XIII

AMENDING THE AMENDING PROCESS

THE very minimum change necessary, if our Constitution is to have any real flexibility, and if any extensive, well-considered reform is even to be made possible, is a change from our present method of constitutional amendment itself.

It is true that one can conceive of extensive amendment to the Constitution without this particular change. Disregarding our original Bill of Rights (the ten amendments adopted as a unit in 1791), we have succeeded in passing eleven amendments to the Constitution in the century and a half since then. Conceivably Congress could frame a lengthy amendment providing for a parliamentary form of government and submit it to the state legislatures or to "conventions" in the present prescribed manner. But the advantages of approaching this goal by two or more steps, rather than by one, seem to me of determining importance, as I shall try later to show.

The present method of amending the Constitution is prescribed in Article V. This is in some respects the most poorly conceived, and certainly the most vague and ambiguous, of all the articles in the Constitution. Let us look at it:

The Congress, whenever two-thirds of both Houses shall deem it necessary, shall propose amendments to this Constitution, or, on the application of the legislatures of two-thirds of the several States, shall call a convention for proposing amendments, which in either case shall be valid to all intents and purposes as part of this Constitution when ratified by the legislatures of three-fourths of the several States, or by conventions in three-fourths thereof, as the one or the other mode of ratification may be proposed by the Congress. . . .

A number of ambiguities become immediately apparent here. No time limit is placed on the period during which two-thirds of the state legislatures may apply for a constitutional convention in order that their application may be valid. Must all two-thirds apply within one year? Two years? Ten years? Can applications remain valid and accumulate over a century? Is a particular state "legislature" in this connection to be defined as the body which bore that name at any time, or solely as the legislature as it has existed since the last legislative election?

It will be noticed, also, that while Congress is to call a convention after two-thirds of the state legislatures ask for it, no time limit is set within which Congress must call this convention. No method is indicated, either, by which the members of this convention are to be chosen. It is not inconceivable that Congress could legally declare *itself* to be the convention. At all events, the ambiguities and pitfalls of this prescribed method of amending the Constitution are so formidable that it has not only never been used, it has never even been seriously contemplated or discussed.

The method used in all but one instance for changes actually adopted has been that of ratification by state legislatures of amendments proposed by Congress. This method has been cumbrous and dilatory. No method is prescribed in Article V by which Congress may compel all the state legislatures to vote at the same time, or with reasonable promptness, or even to vote on proposed amendments at all. As a result, long intervals have chronically elapsed between the submission of amendments and their ratification. It took more than two years for the state legislatures to ratify the original ten amendments, the Bill of Rights, now properly regarded as the most precious part of our Constitution. It took just a little short of four years to ratify the eleventh amendment; nine months to ratify the twelfth; ten months to ratify the thirteenth; more than two years to ratify the fourteenth; thirteen months to ratify the fifteenth; three years and seven months to ratify the sixteenth; one year to ratify the seventeenth; thirteen months to ratify the eighteenth; fourteen months to ratify the nineteenth; eleven months to ratify the twentieth. The child-labor amendment, proposed in 1924, has never been ratified by the States. This applies to other amendments submitted by Congress, dating as far back as 1789. These proposals are presumably dead, and not now subject to action by the state legislatures—though there is nothing in the Constitution that places a time limit on the life of these proposals.

In the latest case in which Congress proposed an amendment, however—that in which it proposed repeal of the eighteenth amendment—it for the first time used the alternative prescribed in the Constitution of submitting the amendment to conventions in the States. It was suddenly discovered (what does not seem until that time to have occurred to anyone) that if the people of the States were asked to choose "delegates" to such "conventions," they would in effect be conventions in name only. For the delegates would be chosen—like those to the Electoral College—simply to record a vote on a single question. In such a case the personalities and other opinions of the delegates become irrelevant. Choosing the delegates for their announced intention of voting yes or no on a single question, the people are in effect deciding the question themselves by direct vote. With the twenty-first amendment, the new method of ratification proved comparatively expeditious. This amendment—which was little more than a repeal of the eighteenth—was ratified less than ten months after Congress submitted it.

There are, however, some serious flaws even in the method of ratification by state "conventions." The Constitution does not specify whether Congress has the power itself to call such conventions, or to force the legislatures to do so, or to prescribe the date when such conventions shall meet or when the people in the States shall elect delegates to them. In the repeal of the eighteenth amendment, Congress assumed that it did not have such powers. It assumed, at all events, that its possession of such powers was so doubtful that it was wisest not to try to exercise them.

It has been argued by some authorities that Congress does have such powers by implication. If Congress may prescribe which of two alternative modes of ratification is to be adopted, may it not also, by implication, prescribe the details of either mode? Certainly the doctrine of implied powers has been stretched much further than this by Supreme Court decisions in other cases.[1]

It is reasonable to assume that Congress has more powers in this direction than it has ever previously chosen to exercise. Its caution hitherto has been doubtless owing to fear of prejudicing state legislatures needlessly against the particular amendment proposed, as well as to fears (even though it may have thought the probabilities in its favor) that the Supreme Court might later declare an amendment invalid on the ground that Congress had gone beyond its powers in prescribing the details of the mode of ratification. But Congress could without risk to a particular amendment proposal use its undoubted prestige in such a matter. In prescribing the method of ratification by conventions, for example, it could *recommend* to the state legislatures the details of the ratification method. Congress could declare in a separate

---

[1] For example, "to regulate commerce ... among the several States" ... "to establish post offices and post-roads" ... "to make all laws which shall be necessary and proper for carrying into execution the foregoing powers, and all other powers vested by this Constitution in the government of the United States, or in any department or office thereof."

joint resolution something like this: "In proposing the mode of ratification by state conventions, the Congress strongly urges that the delegates should be chosen in the following manner," etc. "It urges that the date of election of the delegates to the respective state conventions be uniform throughout the nation, and be fixed by the state legislatures at the next general election on Nov. 3"; or "at a special election on May 15," etc.; and "that the delegates chosen meet throughout the nation at a date not less than two weeks following their election," etc. Such a recommendation should at least have a great moral effect in expediting action on a proposed amendment.

But the ambiguities of Article V remain. The method of submitting proposed amendments to state conventions does not remove these ambiguities, nor does it simplify the amendment process. On the contrary, it actually requires more steps than the submission of amendments direct to the state legislatures. For the state legislatures, in the case of repeal of the eighteenth amendment, prescribed the method of choosing the delegates to the conventions and set the election times, while after the election the delegates chosen had to "convene" and go through the formality of voting on the subject. State legislatures can, if they wish (certainly as long as Congress interprets its powers narrowly on the point), be as dilatory in calling conventions as in voting on an amendment themselves. In either case nothing but public opinion in its own state can force a state legislature to act; and there is no direct machinery for making this public opinion both unmistakable and effective.

2

Our amendment process is not merely cumbersome and dilatory, but altogether uncertain in its working, particularly as regards the time element. If we analyze the historic record, we find that the average time required for the ratification of such proposed amendments as finally were ratified has been about twenty-two months. But that is not the worst of it. For there is no assurance in advance, in proposing an amendment, that it can be ratified in the nine or ten months that it took to ratify the twelfth, thirteenth and twenty-first amendments; it might require the nearly four years of the eleventh amendment.

The child-labor amendment, proposed in 1924, has not, as we have just noticed, been ratified to this day. It was this very situation, indeed, that President Franklin Roosevelt seized upon in his campaign in 1937 to enlarge the Supreme Court. Opponents of that proposal suggested that if the Court were to be reformed, the proper way to do it was to submit the question directly to the people through a constitutional amendment. But the President in his speeches and press conferences pointed to the delays required in the past by the amendment process, especially stressing the fate of the proposed child-labor amendment. The reform he was urging, he argued, could not wait. In a speech on Mar. 4, 1937, he insisted that it must come "Now, Now, Now!" In a "fireside chat" a few days later (Mar. 9), he said:

"I have thus explained to you the reasons that lie behind our efforts to secure results by legislation within the Constitution. I hope that thereby the difficult process of constitutional amendment may be rendered unnecessary.

"It would take months or years," the President went on, "to get substantial agreement upon the type and language of an amendment." This particular argument was without substance. Why should it take longer to agree on the language of an amendment than on the language of a law? His next argument had somewhat more point, though the case was greatly overstated: "It would take months and years thereafter to get a two-thirds majority in favor of that amendment in *both* Houses of the Congress." The President then came to his real case:

"Then would come the long course of ratification by three-fourths of all the States. No amendment which any powerful economic interests or the leaders of any powerful political party have had reason to oppose has ever been ratified within anything like a reasonable time. And thirteen States which contain only five per cent of the voting population can block ratification even though the thirty-five States with ninety-five per cent of the population are in favor of it."

Here the President's argument was substantially correct. But the natural conclusion from it was that the dilatory and uncertain process of amending the

Constitution should itself be amended. Yet though the President had then been in power for four years, he had never made this proposal, nor has he made it in the more than six years since then.

The President concluded: "Now [opponents of my plan] are making a last stand. And the strategy of that last stand is to suggest the time-consuming process of amendment in order to kill off by delay the legislation demanded."

Though the President, through the processes of time and fate, in the end got the substance of what he wanted, which was merely a change in the membership and the particular opinions of the court during his incumbency, Congress refused to pass the legislation on which he had so strongly insisted. It is an ironic reflection that if the President had consented, as he was urged, to submit as an amendment a proposal fixing an obligatory retirement age for Supreme Court justices, the overwhelming probability is that it would long ago have been ratified.

Not the least important reason for making it easier and simpler to amend our Constitution, is that the present inordinate difficulties supply a ready excuse for our officials to urge that instead of submitting amendments directly to the people in a straightforward way, these officials should be permitted to "interpret" the existing Constitution to mean that they already have the new powers that they are seeking. This is a dangerous and a growing tendency. It is not merely in the case of the Supreme Court proposal that the President or members of his Cabinet have urged that the people be by-passed in this manner. There is the proposal, for example, to forbid the issuance of further tax-exempt bonds on the part of the Federal Government, the States and localities. This is in itself a highly desirable reform, properly urged since the income tax became a leading source of revenue. It need hardly be pointed out that if Franklin Roosevelt had urged this at the beginning of his first term, it would undoubtedly already have been in effect, even allowing for highly improbable delays, for at least the last half dozen years. But the Administration keeps attempting to effect this reform without submitting an amendment. (Mr. Morgenthau, the Secretary of the Treasury, has even put forward the inexcusable proposal that outstanding tax-exempt issues of the Federal and local Governments, sold on the basis of their tax-exempt feature, should be taxed by the Federal Government. This would be a clear act of bad faith, apart from any constitutional question whatever.)

Another reform that has been urged by Mr. Roosevelt is one that would permit the President to veto individual items in appropriation bills. This reform is desirable in itself if we are going to retain the presidential system. As we have noted, the Governors of more than three-fourths of the States already possess this power. But Mr. Roosevelt declared in a letter to Senator Vandenberg in March, 1942, that in his opinion no constitutional amendment was necessary to achieve this reform: it could be achieved simply by law. Now this would not be a case of circumventing the Constitution. Clearly Congress could pass a self-denying act granting the President the power to veto individual items in future appropriation bills. But just as clearly almost nothing would be gained by such a law. For the moment the present or any succeeding Congress wished to prevent the President from vetoing a particular appropriation item (as it certainly would), it could include in the bill itself a provision suspending the President's individual-item veto right for that bill and, for that matter, for any future bill. To prevent this the President would have to veto the entire appropriation—a right that he already has.

Clearly, only constitutional amendment can achieve any permanent progress in this and other respects. And clearly, also, the most desirable first step is to simplify the amendment process itself.

3

In the first chapter I suggested that probably the best amendatory method is the one already in use in the Commonwealth of Australia. Amendments to the Constitution of that country may be proposed by a vote of an absolute majority of both the Senate and the House of Representatives. The proposed amendments are then submitted to a direct vote of the people, and adopted if they are approved by a majority of the voters in a majority of the States.

This amendment method could, of course, be modified in detail without changing its substance. Some persons, for example, may prefer to retain our own requirement of a two-thirds vote of both Houses to submit an amendment. I incline to the less stringent

Australian requirement of an absolute majority, on the ground that a minority in either House ought not to be able to hold up the submission of an amendment. But the difference between the absolute majority and the two-thirds requirement seems unlikely to prove very important in practice. The first would doubtless prove nearly as difficult to achieve as the second.

Again, some persons may prefer that ratification be required not only by a majority of the people but by a majority in *two-thirds* of the States. This again seems unlikely to prove an important difference in practice, though what difference there is seems to me to favor the Australian plan. Suppose, for example, that an amendment were to be submitted to the people and were to be approved by a majority of the people in a majority of the States, though it failed to get the approval of a majority in two-thirds of the States. If we adopted the two-thirds requirement, the amendment would be defeated. The country would be almost certain to feel that a minority had been granted excessive veto powers against an approved reform.

The Australian plan seems to me to give all the protection that is really essential. It assures that no amendment will be adopted unless it is wanted by a majority of the people and unless it is wanted in a majority of the States. It protects the country against measures that may be wanted only by the thinly populated States, even if in a majority; and it protects the majority of States against measures wanted only in the great centers of population.

Two other merits of the Australian plan should be emphasized. It allows amendments to be submitted to the direct approval of the people. This is of the first importance. Our present method of submission to "conventions" (which Congress proposed, however, only for the repeal of the eighteenth amendment), is a popular referendum in substance but not in form. It would be simpler and clearer to submit amendments to popular referendum in form as well as substance. It would emphasize the intention to put the Constitution more directly in the control of the people. It would oblige officeholders to seek a clear popular approval for new powers that they wished to exercise. It would discourage their attempts to "interpret" the existing Constitution to mean what they want it to mean.

The other merit of the Australian plan, allied with this, is that it permits a proposed amendment to be submitted to a nation-wide vote on a set date, presumably either the next general election or a special election called by Congress. Obviously Congress itself should have the power to name the date of the vote on the referendum. This would not only expedite the amendment process, but remove all the present possibilities of doubt concerning when an amendment issue will be settled.

In several respects, however, it seems to me desirable to go beyond the Australian plan, and to retain, though in altered form, the two alternative methods of constitutional amendment already provided for in Article V. First, Congress should retain the option of submitting proposed amendments to the legislatures of the States instead of to direct referendum. This would provide for cases in which the proposed amendment was deemed too technical or specialized in nature to be suitable for popular referendum. My own opinion is that even if this option were retained it would almost never be used. Obviously the burden of proof would be upon those in Congress who wished to submit an amendment to state legislatures rather than to the people. But in the case of a purely technical amendment to the Constitution, a popular election might seem merely a needless nuisance and expense. It seems desirable that Congress should retain at least the *right* to submit an amendment to state legislatures. In such a case I suggest that a ratification by two-thirds of the state legislatures (instead of either a mere majority or the present three-fourths) should be required.

The other alternative has to do with the proposal of amendments. It is not healthy that only one body should have this power. One of the most serious problems of democracy is that of legislatures or bureaucracies that have got out of effective control by the people. The people can change the individual legislators at elections, but they cannot reduce their numbers or their prerogatives. Legislatures, no matter with what numbers they may start, always tend in time to outgrow their optimum size. (The French Parliament before the fall of the Third Republic was a notorious example.) In American States or municipalities that are constitutionally required to reapportion their electoral districts or memberships at certain periods, it is a common experience to find that they simply neglect or refuse to do so; and the voters are powerless to do anything about it.

Common sense suggests, and experience has shown, that if a legislative body has the sole power to submit amendments, the amendments it submits will tend steadily in the same direction. It will propose additions to the legislature's own powers, almost never reductions of them. This has been the history of the proposed Australian amendments. Nearly all have been in the direction of centralizing more powers in the Federal Government. This is hardly surprising, when only an agency of the central govenment has the right to propose such amendments. The same tendency has been present in amendments to our own Constitution. I am not here raising the question whether it is desirable to continue the tendency to centralize more power in the Federal at the expense of the state governments. That is a matter for the people to decide regarding this or that specific power. The point I am here making is that a one-way amendment system loads the dice. To prevent the powers and prerogatives of Congress, and of the Federal Government generally, from getting beyond control, the state legislatures should also have the power of proposing amendments.

This they already ostensibly have; but the prescribed method is at once so ambiguous and so full of difficulties that, as we have noted, it has never once been used, or even seriously contemplated. Article V provides that Congress shall call a convention for proposing amendments to the Constitution upon the application of the legislatures of two-thirds of the States. The ambiguities of this provision have already been pointed out earlier in this chapter. In themselves they are almost enough to make the provision unworkable. The sheer arithmetic of the situation does the rest. At the time the Constitution was put into effect, two-thirds of the legislatures meant only nine legislatures. Today it means thirty-two legislatures, consisting of a total of sixty-three houses. These sixty-three houses would not be asked merely to *ratify* a definite proposal submitted by Congress; they would be required spontaneously to *initiate* a proposal. And the proposal would be merely the indefinite one of obliging Congress to call a convention. None of the legislatures would have any idea of what the convention would propose when called. Is it surprising that no such concerted action has ever been taken by the state legislatures?

I suggest that the state legislatures be given the power to propose specific amendments; and that not more than one-quarter of the state legislatures be required to agree on a given amendment for Congress to be obliged to submit it to the people for ratification. Congress would be required so to act within a definite time after the last state legislature (at present this would be the twelfth) had endorsed the amendment. A definite time limit might also be put upon the life of such a proposed amendment if it failed to obtain the endorsement of the necessary number of state legislatures.

To see where these various proposals would leave us, let us try to imagine how an amendment of the amendatory process would read. It might be roughly as follows:

The Congress, whenever an absolute majority of both Houses shall deem it necessary, shall propose amendments to this Constitution. It may submit a proposed amendment for ratification either to the legislatures of the several States or directly to the people of the States. If an amendment is submitted to the state legislatures, it shall become part of this Constitution if ratified by two-thirds of the state legislatures within a period of three years or less of the day of submission. If an amendment is submitted directly to the qualified voters of the states, it shall become part of this Constitution if approved by a majority of all the voters of the nation in a majority of the states. The Congress shall have the power to declare whether such a vote shall be taken at a regular election or at a special election; to fix a uniform national date for such a vote, to appropriate monies for the expense of such a vote, and to prescribe such other details and measures as it may deem necessary in connection therewith.

If one-quarter or more of the legislatures of the several States propose within any period of three years or less an identical amendment to this Constitution, the Congress must submit such an amendment to the people of the States, to be voted upon not more than one year after the required number of legislatures have acted.

Although such an amending provision would allow a comparatively long period during which a proposed amendment would remain legally alive, it would make possible, for the first time in our history, the submission and ratification of an amendment within a period of a few months—or even within a few weeks if Congress thought that an emergency required it.

4

Objections to such an amending provision may come either from those who do not think it goes far enough or from those who think it goes too far. The former may say: "You admit that legislators are highly unlikely to propose amendments that would reduce their own numbers or their own powers, or amendments that would change election methods or districts in such a way as to make less likely their individual chances of reelection. Yet you propose only two alternative sources of amendments, both legislative. It is true that legislators in the individual States have different interests from those of Congressmen, but they also, *as* legislators, have that sense of solidarity of interests, the feeling that 'we must all stick together,' so often found among the members of the same profession. The members of the state legislatures would be unlikely to propose any amendment, to undermine the security or curb the powers of existing members of Congress, which might suggest analogous state amendments to curb their own powers and prerogatives. Why should not the people themselves be permitted to take the initiative in this matter?"

Such a proposal seems to me to have considerable force, but at the same time to present considerable difficulties. The "initiative," as we saw in Chap. VII, is a dangerous device that has worked badly. Laws or amendments framed by a legislative body are often bad enough, but usually, at least, they go through a long process of discussion and refinement. A tentative law or amendment is framed: hearings are held; witnesses point out the effects of this or that provision; the law may be sent to an expert drafting staff; it is debated; amendments are proposed. By this time its possibilities for good or evil have been well examined, and the grosser omissions or oversights corrected. But a law or amendment proposed by petition is usually drafted by amateurs, often by a single amateur, and not uncommonly by a crank or fanatic. It may go through no process of refinement whatever. Yet it may readily lend itself to support by plausible slogans. Worse, a law or amendment framed and adopted by a legislature, if found to work badly or to be defectively drafted, can be changed without inordinate difficulty. But a law or amendment adopted by both initiative and referendum, as we have seen, is extremely difficult to alter by the same process, and acquires such a sacrosanct quality through its method of adoption that a mere legislature fears on its own motion to lay hands even on a comma of it.

I suggested in Chap. VII that we might provide for adoption of amendments by popular initiative and obligatory referendum if we confined the use of this method to amendments designed only to *reduce* the numbers, terms or powers of legislators or to change their method of election or basis of representation. The question to be raised here, however, is whether it would be possible to keep the use of this method within the bounds intended. Petitions would undoubtedly be circulated that attempted to combine such a reform with others. Should Congress itself be granted the legal right to declare such petitions invalid? Would it have the courage to do so? Would a useful purpose be served by granting the right of the initiative, but giving Congress the power to amend or redraft such petitions as had received the necessary signatures? These questions are difficult. It would seem wise to begin with a reformed amendment process to the Constitution that did not go so far as to include such a method. This would make it much easier to achieve the immediate reforms that are more clearly needed; and it would not bar later consideration of this additional method.

There is another direction in which the changes in the amending process that I have suggested may not be deemed to go far enough. They do not provide either immediately or ultimately for calling a convention to frame a new constitution. Even the existing amendatory clause provides, it may be contended, by however awkward and improbable a method of initiation, for the calling of a constitutional convention to propose amendments to the constitution.

I confess I can see no strong objection to any proposal to revise the Constitution by calling a convention. But several observations may be made about such a proposal. First, if we make the amendment process itself simple and expeditious, then we can at any time pass an amendment calling for such a constitutional convention. But there is no magic in a constitutional convention. The reasons in favor of such a convention are less compelling than many persons may suppose. To begin with, it is not necessary to call a constitutional convention to revise the Constitution completely rather than merely to "amend" it. Some writers seem to believe that "amendment" necessarily implies mere patchwork in minor respects, and does not permit of thorough revision. But such writers overlook the everyday procedure of Congress, in which the Senate, "amending" a revenue bill originating in the House, strikes out everything after the title of the bill and writes an entirely different document. In the same way, an "amendment" to the Constitution could be proposed that would strike out everything after the paragraph "We the people . . . do ordain and establish this Constitution." This amendment could be in itself an entirely new Constitution, and, if it were ratified by popular referendum, "we the people" would indeed be ordaining and establishing a Constitution in a far more literal sense than did "the people" of 1789.

Since in either case it is the people who would be called upon to approve a proposed revision of the Constitution, the real question is whether such a revision would be framed by Congress or by a special convention. There is no reason to suppose in advance that the membership of such a convention would necessarily be superior to that of Congress. In any case, the convention would be unlikely to begin, any more than Congress, by acting as a full body: it would appoint committees and subcommittees to study special aspects of the problem and draft proposals for discussion. In this respect a continuing Congress would have an advantage over a specially called convention; its committees would be able to act with less haste; they would not be delaying a large body that could not otherwise proceed. It may be pointed out, further, that it would not be necessary for Congress to begin such a study with its own members: it might appoint a special expert commission of non-members to frame a revised constitution to submit to Congress. (The New Jersey legislature recently created by joint resolution just such a commission—the seven-member Commission on Revision of the New Jersey Constitution.)

The advantages that a special constitutional convention might have over Congress as a revising body are mainly three: (1) it would devote its entire time to such revision, without the distraction of having meanwhile to pass upon ordinary legislation; (2) its members would be chosen presumably for their special interest in constitutional questions, even if they lacked special qualifications for dealing with such questions; (3) and most important, the members of a special constitutional convention would not have the same vested interests in certain parts of the existing Constitution that the members of Congress might have. I can imagine the members of Congress proposing a

Constitution that would give them power to force the resignation of the executive. But would they be equally ready to give the executive power to order a dissolution of Congress and a new election?

These considerations might be felt to determine the question in favor of a constitutional convention that could submit its results directly to the people for approval and not to Congress. This would be the case for retaining in a revised amendatory section the existing provision that Congress must call a constitutional convention upon the application of the legislatures of two-thirds of the States, or inserting a provision compelling Congress to do so if it received petitions with a sufficient number of signatures. (In a case of this sort, which called for a general action without attempting to specify details, the initiative would retain its possible advantages without its serious handicaps.)

If the state legislatures could be brought to act under the present Constitution, they could take a great forward step immediately. But they would be likely to act only if public opinion reached a critical stage as a result of some great setback in the war, and if one state legislature assumed a bold and effective leadership. It is only because the psychological and political obstacles to such action through the state legislatures seem so great, that I have recommended the intermediate step of an amendment of the amending process before undertaking a more extensive direct revision of the Constitution. The great advantage of amending the amending process is that it can be done without at all affecting the existing balance of powers or functions or the existing government personnel. It can therefore be done without even an implied criticism of any governmental group. It would clear the way for later changes; but no one could argue that in itself it did anything at all to "disrupt existing institutions" in a period of crisis.

Only one serious objection seems likely to be offered to the amendment of the amending process here proposed. It is that it would make it "too easy" to alter the Constitution, and so lead to frivolous or ill-considered changes. But this has not proved to be true in Australia, which has this type of amendatory provision. Since the adoption of the Australian Constitution, the people of that country have accepted only three of the eighteen proposals for amendment submitted by the Australian Parliament.

The argument that we should not make it simpler for ourselves to amend our national Constitution, for fear that we may only make it worse, is a form of self-distrust that, if warranted, would logically lead us to abandon our democratic principles altogether. Amendments should, of course, be well considered; but mere arbitrary delays, mere hurdles of political machinery, cannot in themselves force us to think better. To the argument that such artificial hurdles and delays reduce the likelihood of error, the obvious reply is that they also make it more difficult to correct errors. It was the difficulty of amending our Constitution (and the supposed impossibility of amending it by a direct vote of the people) that kept Prohibition fastened on the country long after the majority of voters had become disgusted with it.

We return to the verdict of Bryce that I have quoted before: "The process of amending the Constitution is so troublesome that even a change which involves no party issues may remain unadopted long after the best opinion has become unanimous in its favor."[1] Errors in constitutional change are not likely to prove too serious if they can be easily corrected. We may sometimes learn more through actual experience of changes than through the most brilliant *a priori* thinking by political philosophers regarding their probable effects.

The present writer has yet to meet anyone, no matter how conservative or how much opposed to the general notion of constitutional change, who does not, when questioned, approve *some* change in our Constitution. Sometimes this takes the disguised form of wishing to get everyone else to accept his own particular *interpretation* of the Constitution. For those who wish to make their particular interpretation of a constitutional clause prevail over rival interpretations, there is a candid way to go about it. They can propose that their interpretation be submitted as an explicit amendment, so that the country can directly make it clear whether or not it wishes that interpretation to prevail. If they are unwilling to do this, we must conclude that, under the pretense of believing that no amendment is needed, they wish to impose their own amendment by subterfuge.

[1] *The American Commonwealth*, Vol. I, p. 215.

Let us put the matter on a straightforward basis. Let those who are willing to take no other step at all at least agree now to simplify the amending process so that, without needless delays, amendments may be submitted directly to the people. Once this is done, we shall be in a position to consider constitutional revision realistically, and with clear minds.

XIV

CONCLUSION

ONCE we have recognized the vices of our form of government, we must act to remove them. This does not mean a generation hence, or in the next decade, or next year. We must begin *now*. The issue of victory or defeat may hang on a narrow margin: we cannot afford deliberately to handicap ourselves by adhering to a form of government that we recognize to be dangerously inefficient or unreliable in a crisis.

What is the central vice of our form of government? In a single word, it is *irresponsible*. All its chief defects come back to this. Either they are forms of irresponsibility, or they promote it. We arbitrarily separate the legislature and the executive. We choose each in such a way that there is no assurance that they will want the same policies—indeed, often in such a way that it is almost certain that they will want different policies. Congress can prevent the President from doing what he wishes, but cannot make him do what it wishes. The President, through his veto power, can usually prevent Congress from doing as it wishes unless its desired policy is almost unanimous. He needs only the support of "a third plus one" in *one* House of the legislature to stop Congress from adopting a policy. Moreover, if he does not like a law that Congress adopts, he may enforce it either very feebly or in such a way as to make it seem obnoxious. If the President wishes any positive action from Congress, he must usually get his way, as Harold Laski has put it, "very largely by the use of patronage—about as undesirable a method of persuasion as the imagination can conceive."[1] The Senate, again—indeed, a single Senate committee chairman unknown to the public—may through negative vote or mere inaction absolutely veto even the unanimous will of the House of Representatives.

The result is hopelessly to confuse the public regarding whom to hold responsible for a policy or for failure to adopt a policy. The public must wait perhaps through years of deadlock and paralysis to decide the question by its vote; and assuming even then that it knows *how* to decide, it may be powerless to decide. It cannot change whom it wishes when it wishes. It cannot change the government, or the government's policies, at any one election. At one election it can change the House of Representatives but not the President; so that even if it strongly disapproves of the President's policies it must nevertheless either endorse those policies or create a stalemate. At no election can it change more than one-third of the Senate. And if the voters of the whole country are almost unanimous in their opposition, say, to the influential foreign policies of the chairman of the Senate Foreign

[1] *Parliamentary Government in England* (1938), p. 139.

CONCLUSION

Relations Committee (who gets his position, not by the free choice of his colleagues, but by seniority), they are powerless to do anything about it. Only the voters of a single State—the State from which the Senator comes (at the present moment, Texas, representing less than 5 per cent of the total voting population), are ever consulted on that question, and then only once in six years.

All this makes for government irresponsibility of the most shocking kind. The only cure is the adoption of the principle of *concentration of responsibility*. This, as Ramsay Muir has pointed out, is the essential principle of the British Constitution, as contrasted with the *separation of powers* which is still the basic principle of the American Constitution.[1]

Since the attack on Pearl Harbor the American public has been brought to recognize how disastrous can be the consequences of failure to fix and concentrate responsibility, even in the lower echelons of command. The Pearl Harbor disaster itself, in which the war was nearly lost in a day, was in large part owing, as the Roberts Commission report made clear, to the failure to concentrate responsibility for the defense of Pearl Harbor. Authority was divided between the Army and Navy commanders there; neither seemed to know exactly where his responsibility began or ended: neither was under obligation to consult with the other regarding the question; and so neither, apparently, condescended to consult the other. When the *Normandie*, the greatest shipping

[1] *How Britain Is Governed* (1929), p. 21.

prize in the hands of the American Government, was burned at its pier through inexcusable carelessness, an investigation by Congress revealed no one whose authority had been so unmistakably fixed in advance that he could be held clearly responsible for the disaster. When Congress tried to find who was responsible for the Government's failure to build up a great stock pile of rubber and to begin effective steps to encourage synthetic production, it was confronted by more efforts to shift responsibility. At the time of writing there is no way to determine who was responsible for the failure to have sufficient air power at the Philippines or to protect that air power from almost instant destruction. Even the broadest facts necessary to form a judgment have been withheld from the public.

If these are the results of failure to fix and concentrate responsibility at lower levels, what must be said of our national failure to fix and concentrate responsibility at the very top? American officeholders are in the habit of using the word "responsibility" very loosely. They often declare roundly that they "take full responsibility" for this or that step; but they fail to recognize the implications of their statement. Responsibility implies, in public life, *accountability;* and real accountability implies *immediate removability*. There is no other political way in which responsibility can be made effective. We make a general in the field responsible in two ways: we give him the men, the equipment, the help and the full authority he asks for; we honor him for his success; and we re-

CONCLUSION

move him for his failure. So it should be with our political leaders. We should not place in power with them other men who conceive it to be their duty or function to obstruct them at every turn. We should clothe them with real authority for positive as well as negative action. But if they fail to carry out the wishes of the people, then the people, without long or disastrous delays, should be able to remove them.

Because America does not follow this policy, its public thought is hopelessly and chronically confused. We sink into endless argument over points that in England could not be the subject of argument at all. Who was responsible for American unpreparedness? This was a subject of dispute in the Presidential election of 1940 and has been since. We "analyze" the votes of Republicans and Democrats on a score or more of bills. In practically no case do we find a solid vote of Republicans opposed to a solid vote of Democrats; we decide in each case by comparing the percentage division of the vote within each party. (The Republicans alone, in fact, could not at any time have blocked a single "Administration" measure. Whenever the majority of Republicans was successful, it was through the aid of recalcitrant Democrats.) Who was responsible for the original Neutrality Bill? Was the President "forced" to sign this against his judgment? Who blocked the proposal for the fortification of Guam? What defense appropriations were the Republicans mainly responsible for blocking? What of the defense appropriations that the President never even asked for? What attitude *would* the Republicans have taken, or would "Congress" have taken, if these appropriations *had* been asked for?

Few questions of this sort could ever arise in England, or in any country with a sound cabinet government. The Prime Minister or a member of his Cabinet would state his preparedness policy and ask for his appropriation. If Parliament refused that appropriation, or attempted to cut it down, or tried to pass any neutrality bill in spite of "the Government's" wishes, the Prime Minister could announce that the vote was a vote of confidence, and could resign or dissolve Parliament if it failed to meet his wishes. The public would never have the slightest doubt as to where responsibility lay. It might have the opportunity then and there, in fact, to decide between the Prime Minister and the parliamentary majority, if the two disagreed, and to make unmistakably known its own ideas of what the proper policy should be. *That* is responsible government.

It is a defect of the presidential system not merely that it scatters responsibility within the government itself among separate agencies insulated from each other, but that it has no organized opposition. This may seem a strange defect to complain of; nevertheless, it is a real and a serious one. "He who wrestles with us," wrote Burke, "strengthens our nerves, and sharpens our skill. Our antagonist is our helper." A good opposition forces a government to improve itself.

When there is no organized opposition, the criticism of the government's policies is the random and sporadic criticism of individuals as such. They are all saying different things; most of them are ill informed; they are only a babble of voices; they are likely to sound like mere carpers and scolders; and the public is confused. One criticism is often the opposite of another. The government seizes upon this fact, argues that the two criticisms cancel out, and that they prove it must be doing a good job. When individual Congressmen of the opposite party speak only for themselves, each says only those particular things that he thinks will help toward his own reelection in his own district. Criticism under presidential government is commonly aimless, moreover, because except at fixed intervals of four years no immediate result can follow from it.

But under a cabinet form of government the opposition is as organized as the government itself. It has a chosen leader. That leader is its spokesman. That leader must consult his colleagues, just as the premier must, and formulate a responsible program of criticism. The criticism is that of a party eager to prove that it is itself able to take over the government, if need be, at once. The leader of the opposition must therefore forego trivial and carping criticisms, which merely confuse the public, and concentrate on those issues that are centrally important. He must propose some constructive alternative to the course that he condemns. The criticism by an organized opposition, in brief, is not scattered and self-contradictory, but unified and consistent. The public is educated by this clarity. The opposition can itself help to frame issues.

It can force the government to take a position on them. In Britain these vital functions are acknowledged. "His Majesty's Opposition" is recognized to be an integral part of the governmental system.

Responsibility, I have said, implies immediate removability. By that I mean immediate removability either of the chief executive himself, or of those in the legislature whose votes have effectively opposed him. It is not difficult to see why this must be so. If the executive's opponents in the legislature cannot be immediately removed by the people, they can continue to oppose his will and make it impossible for him fully to carry out his policies. In that case he cannot be held clearly responsible if the results are bad. If the chief executive himself, on the other hand, cannot be immediately removed when he is unable or unwilling to carry out the popular will, then the people in the interim before removal have a government that is not responsible to them because they cannot reach it. The absence of this immediate removability perverts public thought, for when the people know in advance that they cannot change their executive even when they are dissatisfied with him, they hesitate to hold him clearly responsible for his errors lest they discredit him at home and abroad and bring about a situation of mere chaos.

So difficult has it been under our system to fix responsibility, and so reluctant has the public been even to try to fix responsibility for disaster on men in high places whom it has no means of removing, that a strange doctrine has been preached in America. This doctrine tells us that we were "all of us responsible" for our general unpreparedness, for the loss of the Philippines, or for the disaster at Pearl Harbor. It is not necessary here to try to weigh elaborately the pros and cons of this remarkable contention. It is sufficient to notice that the notion of *universal* responsibility in such a context is a "non-operational" concept.[1] That is to say, it is meaningless for practical action; nothing can be done with it.

The dictionary tells us that responsible means *answerable;* this implies answerable *to* someone. A whole people cannot be operationally answerable to themselves. They cannot replace themselves. They cannot resign, if only because they do not know what to resign *from.* The notion of universal responsibility, in short, is in this context operationally meaningless. It is a vague rhetorical mumble jumble in place of realistic analysis. The notion of the responsibility of specific officials, on the other hand, makes sense. It is an operational concept: one can act on it. If a specific official does well, he can be applauded, promoted or reelected; if he does badly, he can be removed and replaced by someone else who we hope will do better. That is what responsibility really means.

We Americans are usually acknowledged to be the most efficient people in the world as individuals. But we allow ourselves to be organized, or, rather, disorganized, at the top by one of the most miserably in-

---

[1] For a fuller explanation of this phrase, see P. W. BRIDGMAN, *The Logic of Modern Physics*, and the same author's *The Intelligent Individual and Society*, Chap. II.

efficient forms of government that it would be possible to conceive. This inefficiency is dangerous always; in time of war it may prove fatal. Our form of government will become increasingly dangerous to our national welfare and security until we reform it in accordance with the principle of Concentration of Responsibility. What that principle implies in detail I have endeavored to show in the preceding pages.

2

Anyone who has participated in political controversy knows how difficult it is to keep the discussion on a rational plane. The objectivity of science seems almost nowhere. Particularly of late years, there has been an increasingly frequent resort to purely *ad hominem* argument. Instead of examining a proposal on its merits, which is the only rational course, people express suspicions concerning the "source" of the proposal or the motives of its author. Inevitably, many persons will judge a proposal like the present one by its presumable effect on the immediate fortunes of certain political groups. I can only hope that a larger number will be willing to judge it from a broader perspective.

The main purpose of the type of cabinet government here suggested is to make our government more efficient, more responsible, and more responsive to the national will. The real question to be asked, therefore, is whether it will really do this. Men of different parties and different economic philosophies can unite, I hope, in their answer. Supporters of the Administra-

CONCLUSION

tion, feeling confident of the President's great popularity, may favor cabinet government because it would permit Mr. Roosevelt at all times to make his policies effective, by placing in his hands the great weapon of dissolution, or the threat of it, to bring recalcitrant Congressmen into line. Opponents of the present Administration, if they believe that Mr. Roosevelt has so badly mismanaged the war effort that the people will want to change him, may favor for that reason a Constitution that permits them to do so. But the question of Constitutional reform should be judged, not by its possible effect on the immediate fortunes of any individual, party, or group, but on the much wider basis of its effect on the welfare of the whole country, both now and in the longer future. Let us trust that it will have the fortune to be so judged.

3

I must add one postscript. I have urged in this book that a radical revision of our Constitution is a measure essential to the proper conduct of the war, and that if such a revision does not make the difference between losing and winning the war, it will certainly make a difference in the length and cost of the war. If, as most of us confidently believe, we are ultimately to win the war in any case, it is still true that our divided and irresponsible constitutional set-up must prolong the struggle with needless cost in lives and treasure, and that constitutional reform would shorten the war and save those lives and that treasure.

But if, happily, the war is quickly brought to a successful conclusion in spite of the inflexible and disintegrate nature of our governmental framework, it would be deeply unfortunate if it were then supposed that any need for constitutional reform had passed. On the contrary, it would still be imperative, if the democracies are not once more, as in 1918 and 1919, to win the war and lose the peace. The disaster of the Senate's rejection of the League of Nations, and of our withdrawal into a stupid isolationism, repudiating our own participation in the First World War and all that it had cost us, must not be repeated. But that or some equal stupidity is very likely to be repeated unless we fuse the legislature and the executive, concentrate responsibility, and allow our chosen leader to speak with undivided authority to other nations.

After this war, to do this will be more necessary than ever before in our history, more necessary than ever before in world history. Unless some form of international organization and control is adopted, the situation will be intolerable. The peoples in each nation, even when technically at "peace," will live in hourly dread of some tremendous, unannounced, sudden air raid, destroying their ships and military forces and laying waste their cities, like the lightning German attacks on Poland, Norway, Holland, Belgium and Russia, and the Japanese attack on Pearl Harbor. The modern military airplane has put a tremendous premium on treachery. No nation will know what other nation to trust; for the nation that is planning to strike may be precisely the one to give least advance warning through belligerent demands.

CONCLUSION

Anything will be preferable to this—even some limitation on the hitherto absolute sovereignty of individual nations! However "impractical" it may seem, therefore, we must establish some form of preventive control over would-be aggressor nations, some form of international policing, some form of collective security. If we do not move toward world federation, we must at least move away from world division.

The obstacles to such a reform will in any case be tremendous. Let us not increase them by maintaining a disintegrate government for which no one is authorized to speak—because someone else may veto his warnings or his commitments. Let us not repeat the tragedy of Woodrow Wilson and the Senate. Let us adopt responsible cabinet government. Let us *trust* somebody, and give him authority as long as he remains in power; but make him at all times strictly accountable for his use of that power, and removable the moment he shows himself unwilling or incompetent to carry out the national will.

BIBLIOGRAPHY

BAGEHOT, WALTER: *The English Constitution*, World's Classics ed., Oxford University Press, New York, 1867.

BAKER, RAY STANNARD: *Woodrow Wilson and World Settlement*, Doubleday, Doran & Company, Inc., New York, 1922.

BRYCE, JAMES: *The American Commonwealth*, 1931 ed., The Macmillan Company, New York, 1888.

DOWLING, NOEL T.: "Amending the Amending Process," *The Independent Journal of Columbia University*, New York, Feb. 11, 1938.

ELLIOTT, W. Y.: *The Need for Constitutional Reform*, Whittlesey House (McGraw-Hill Book Company, Inc.), New York, 1935.

HERMENS, F. A.: *Democracy or Anarchy?: A Study of Proportional Representation*, University of Notre Dame, Notre Dame, Ind., 1941.

KENT, FRANK R., *The Great Game of Politics*, Doubleday, Doran & Company, Inc., New York, 1923.

LASKI, HAROLD J.: *The American Presidency:* Harper & Brothers, New York, 1940.

LASKI, HAROLD J.: "The American Political System," *The Dangers of Obedience*, Harper & Brothers, New York, 1930.

MACDONALD, WILLIAM: *A New Constitution for a New America*, B. W. Huebsch, Inc., New York, 1921.

McKee, Henry S.: *Degenerate Democracy*, The Thomas Y. Crowell Company, New York, 1933.

Mill, John Stuart: *Representative Government*, Everyman's ed., E. P. Dutton & Company, Inc., New York, 1861.

Millspaugh, Arthur C.: *Democracy, Efficiency, Stability*, Brookings Institution, Washington, D. C., 1942.

Muir, Ramsay: *How Britain Is Governed*, Houghton Mifflin Company, Boston, 1935.

Stolper, Gustav: *This Age of Fable*, pp. 354-358. Reynal & Hitchcock, Inc., New York, 1941.

Wilson, Woodrow: *Congressional Government*, Houghton Mifflin Company, Boston, 1885.

INDEX

A

Acceptance, majority, 194-199
Adams, John Quincy, 216
Administrative agencies, 181-183
Aikman, Duncan, 17
Amendatory procedure, 11-14, 172*ff*., 202, 251-276
Arthur, President, 228
Australia, Constitution of, 11, 12, 261-263, 265, 274
Axelsson, George, 71

B

Bagehot, Walter, 17*ff*., 44, 65-66, 74-75, 78-79, 84, 122, 129, 131*n*., 152, 167, 200, 291
Baker, Ray Stannard, 223-224, 291
Baldwin, Prime Minister, 168
Balfour, Lord, 17
Bentham, Jeremy, 95-96, 184-185
Berdahl, Clarence A., 35*n*.

Bill of Rights, 8, 108, 251, 253
Bonds, tax-exempt, 260
Brazil, 17*n*.
Bridgman, P. W., 285*n*.
British Prime Ministers, tenure of, 62
Bruening, Chancellor, 70
Bryce, James, 3, 5, 32-35, 83-84, 98, 202, 211-212, 217-218, 275, 291
Bucklin voting system, 191-192, 196
Burke, Edmund, 282
Butler, Bishop, 55

C

Cabinet, 18, 131*ff*.
Canadian Prime Ministers, tenure of, 75
Cassel, Gustav, 185-187
"Checks and balances," 31, 239
Child-labor amendment, 253, 257
Childs, Richard S., 234
Churchill, Winston, 6, 213
Citizens Budget Commission, 238

Citizens Emergency Committee on Nondefense Expenditures, 225
Citizens Union, 238
City governments, 233-237
City-manager plan, 49-50, 233-237, 238
Civil War, the, 35-36, 41
Cobb, Frank I., 40-43
Committees, Congressional, 241-248
  legislative, 140-144, 244-247
Concentration of responsibility, 264-267, 277-286
Congress, internal organization of, 241-250
  residential requirement for, 210-217
Constitutional Convention, of 1787, 29, 31
  special, 270-273
Coolidge, 114*n.*, 228
Council, legislative, 133-139, 248-249
Council-manager plan, 49-50, 233-237, 238
Cox, James M., 214

D

Davis, John W., 214
Dawes, Charles G., 214
Debt limit, national, 76

Dewey, Thomas E., 214-215
Dies, Martin, 189, 190
Dowling, Noel T., 291

E

Economist, London, 45, 51-53
Eighteenth Amendment, 254, 256, 263, 274-275
Electoral College, 204, 227, 254
Elliott, W. Y., XI, 99, 291

F

Federal office holders, 113-118, 206-208
Fillmore, President, 227
Foreign Policy Association, 238
France, government of, under Third Republic, 59-67, 74-75, 83, 102-103, 190, 236, 264
French cabinets, duration of, 61

G

Gallup poll, 159
Galveston, Texas, "commission plan," 233-234
Garner, John Nance, 214
Germany, government of,

INDEX

under Weimar Republic, 67*ff.*
Gideonse, Harry D., 120

H

Hallett, G. H., 155*n.*, 193
Hambloch, Ernest, 17*n.*
Hay, John, 223
Heaton, John L., 40
Hermens, F. A., 69*n.*, 70-71, 291
Hindenburg, President, 68, 125
Hitler, 68, 70-71, 125, 168, 230
Hoag, C. G., 155*n.*, 193
Hoover, Herbert, 214

I

Initiative, 157, 158-159, 269-270
Italy, parliamentary government in, 68-69

J

Johnson, Lyndon B., 189, 190, 192
Johnson, President, 228

K

Kent, Frank R., 291
King, Mackenzie, 75

L

Landon, Alfred M., 214
Laski, Harold J., 43-45, 54, 98, 108, 110*n.*, 167, 200-201, 213-214, 223, 278, 291
Latin-American dictatorships, 17, 152, 226
League for Constitutional Reform, 238-240
League of Nations, 34-35, 223, 288
Legislative councils, 133-139, 248-249
Legislature, organization of, 144-157, 165-171, 241-247
Lewis, Sir George, 131
Lincoln, President, 31

M

Macaulay, 96-97
MacDonald, William, 36-37, 39-40, 103-104, 291
McKee, Henry S., 292
Madison, James, 8, 20
Majority acceptance voting, 194-199
Majority preferential voting systems, 191*ff.*
Mann, Gerald, 189, 190
Marx, Karl, 54-56
Mencken, H. L., 212

Mill, John Stuart, 16, 72, 111-113, 117-119, 144-146, 149-150, 184-185, 292
Millspaugh, Arthur C., 173*n*., 292
Montesquieu, 20
Morgenthau, Henry, Jr., 260
Muir, Ramsay, 127, 147*n*., 279, 292
Munro, William B., 234
Mussolini, 69, 71, 125

N

National Economy League, 238
National Municipal League, 238
Nebraska, legislature of, 231
Neutrality Acts, 75-76, 281
New Jersey Constitution, Commission on Revision of the, 272
Norris, Senator George W., 206-207, 231

O

O'Daniel, W. Lee, 189, 190, 192
Opposition, government, 282-284
"His Majesty's Opposition," 284

P

Pearl Harbor, 6, 13, 279, 285, 288
Peel, Sir Robert, 127
Pitt, William, 120
"Polish veto," 174
Price, Don K., 234*n*.
Prohibition, 254, 256, 263, 274-275
Proportional Representation, 68-71, 133-134, 152, 155, 156, 193, 236-237
Putney, Bryant, 248*n*.

R

Recall, 157, 159-164
Referendum, 157-158, 263, 269, 271
Residential requirement, 210-217
Responsibility, concentration of, 264-267, 277-286
Roberts Commission Report, 6, 279
Rogers, Lindsay, 159*n*.
Roosevelt, Franklin D., VII, X, 87, 114*n*., 204, 217, 257-261, 286-287
Roosevelt, Theodore, 228
Root, Elihu, 85
Russell, Bertrand, 55

INDEX

S

Senate, appropriations, 224-226
   basis of representation, 173
   ratification of treaties, 222-224
Senning, John P., 231*n*.
Separation of powers, 18*ff*., 34, 100-106, 210, 219, 279
Sherman, Roger, 29
Smith, Alfred E., 214
Smith, Sydney, 95-96
State constitutions, 229-232
State legislatures, 263-268, 273
Stearns, Harold E., 213*n*.
Stolper, Gustav, 292
Supreme Court, 87-89, 217-221, 255, 257-259

T

Tardieu, Premier, 64
Texas election, 189-190, 192
Third term, 204-210
Tyler, President, 227

V

Vandenberg, Senator, 260
Veto, executive, 210, 224, 260-261, 277
Vice-President, 226-229
Voters, qualifications for, 109-119
Voting, Bucklin system of, 191-192
   majority acceptance system, 194-199
   majority preferential systems, 191*ff*.
   methods of, 188-199
   proportional representation, 68-71, 133-134, 152, 155, 156, 193

W

Wage-Hour act, 243
Wagner labor relations act, 243
Willkie, Wendell, 114*n*., 207, 214
Wilson, Woodrow, X, 28-32, 223-224, 241-243, 244, 289, 292
World federation, 288-289